An Illustrated History

CANADA'S WARS

Jonathan Webb

Foreword by J.L. Granatstein

A SCHOLASTIC/MADISON LESTER EDITION

CONTENTS

A Canadian soldier on patrol in Kandahar Province, Afghanistan, shakes hands with an Afghan boy.

FOREWORD

Canadians today believe that they are peacekeepers; indeed, they think they are the world's very best peacekeepers. After all, they say, External Affairs minister Lester Pearson invented the concept at Suez in 1956, and for years after that, Canadian troops were involved in almost every United Nations peace operation. Canadians served in the Middle East, in the Congo, in Cyprus, in Haiti and Latin America, and in West Irian (New Guinea). Everywhere the United Nations went, Canadian servicemen and women put on the UN's blue berets and represented Canada's commitment to peace with devotion and skill.

Yes, Canadians are peacekeepers. But Canada is something else as well. Canada is a nation that has been shaped by war—war between the French and the Iroquois, between the French and the English, between the English and the Americans, and between Canadians and Louis Riel's Métis. Battles south of Montreal, at Quebec, and along the Niagara frontier decided whether or not Canada would survive and fixed its boundaries. Canadian settlement of the West proceeded only after the government's successful suppression of the 1885 Northwest Rebellion. And war defined the linguistic and even the religious makeup of Canada.

Then there were the two world wars of the 20th century. These titanic struggles determined the fate of great empires and, most important, the survival of democracy and freedom. Raising huge armies and dispatching them overseas, Canadians found to their surprise that they could be warriors. Paying a terrible price in blood and treasure, the Canadian Corps in the First World War and the First Canadian Army in the Second World War demonstrated that this young country's fighters could more than hold their own against the best armies on earth. Canadian seamen and pilots also earned high praise for their skill and daring in both wars, and these hard-earned reputations were enhanced in Korea, the United Nation's first war or "police action," from 1950 to 1953.

What makes this record especially meaningful is that, almost alone among the nations on earth, Canada did not fight to expand its territory or to acquire riches or for glory. Canadians went to war for the best reasons—to protect their people and their territory; to help their friends fend off aggressor states; and to protect and advance freedom and democracy. Some wars are evil in every respect, but when Canadians fought, they did so for selfless reasons, for the best of reasons.

Yes, Canadians are peacekeepers, and Canada's record here is a very good one. But so too is Canada's record in a growing number of armed UN blue-helmet operations that verge on all-out war. Since the end of the Cold War in the early 1990s, United Nations operations have become more difficult: peacekeeping has become peace enforcement, and Canadian and other troops have frequently had to use their weapons. This is true in Somalia and in the former Yugoslavia, where Canadians fought pitched battles. In Afghanistan, an operation authorized by the United Nations but carried out largely under the direction of the United States and the North Atlantic Treaty Organization, Canadian soldiers have spent a decade fighting terrorists in a brutal war seemingly without end.

The world of today, much like the world of the past, is complex and difficult, and unfortunately it probably always will be. What matters for Canada and Canadians is that we continue to use our judgment, committing our men and women to fight only for the right causes. In our nation's life of almost 150 years, we have done that. Canada's wars have been the right ones, and Jonathan Webb's fine volume tells us how Canadians performed on the battlefields and in peace operations.

J.L. Granatstein

SOME MILITARY TERMS

Armour: A shield, usually made of steel, to protect soldiers from bullets and shrapnel. An armoured unit travels in shielded vehicles, typically tanks, armoured personnel carriers, and self-propelled artillery.

Artillery: Big guns that are operated by a crew and typically mounted on wheels, tracks, or a platform of some kind. Artillery includes cannons, rockets, and (nowadays) surface-to-air missiles.

Battery: A fortified position for heavy guns.

Beachhead: The zone seized and held by an armed force attacking a coast.

Commando unit: A group of soldiers specially trained to carry out hit-and-run raids against enemy positions.

Fusillade: Heavy and continuous gunfire.

Guerrillas: Groups of armed individuals who attack regular forces by using hit-and-run tactics, such as sabotage and ambushes, to make up for their smaller number and lack of heavy weapons.

Infantry: Soldiers who march and fight on foot.

Merchant navy: The fleet of ships that carry commercial cargo in a time of war. Merchant sailors are civilians.

Mortar: A portable weapon (essentially a tube supported by two or three legs) that lobs an explosive shell over a relatively short distance.

Reconnaissance: A patrol unit sent to survey enemy positions in advance of an attack.

Self-propelled gun: A shielded cannon mounted on a tracked vehicle. Unlike a tank, it is not meant for front-line combat.

Signals unit: A unit whose job it is to set up and maintain communication between front-line troops and their command centre.

Squadron: In the air force, a squadron contains 12 to 24 aircraft divided into flights. In the navy, a squadron is a group of warships whose number may vary.

Tank: A big gun mounted on an armoured vehicle and designed for front-line combat. The Sherman tank, which was most commonly used by Canadian forces in the Second World War, carried a 75-mm cannon, a 50-mm machine gun, and a crew of five.

HOME FREE

Canada may be the luckiest nation in the world.

The country was originally a collection of colonies, and its first battles were fought by other nations' troops. A British general, James Wolfe, confronted a French general, the Marquis de Montcalm, on the Plains of Abraham in 1759. British armies fought with Americans in the War of 1812. Settlers and Native peoples played only a small part in these struggles. For the colonists, war was often other people's business.

The United States thought about invading the British colonies when their Civil War ended, but never did. Canadians were left to build a nation in peace. Confederation was a deal made by politicians, not soldiers. (The first president of the United States, in contrast, was a general.) Canada is one of a handful of nations that has never really been attacked. A few hundred Irish nationalists—Fenians—raided Niagara and the Quebec border in the late 1860s. A German U-boat sank ships near Halifax in the First World War, also known as the Great War. U-boats did serious damage to shipping in the St. Lawrence River a quarter-century later. While these incidents were alarming, Canada itself was never in danger.

Canada has had a militia (part-time soldiers) since the beginning. In the periods between wars, it has not needed a large, permanent army, navy, or air force. As a result, Canada's forces often have been neglected. Being lucky has allowed it to be thrifty when it comes to the military. And yet, in spite of Canada's mainly peaceful origins, war has played a huge part in our nation's story.

READY, AYE, READY

Canada, after Confederation in 1867, was one small part of the mighty British Empire. When it came to defence, the Canadian government took advice from London. Since most Canadians (nearly 60 per cent in 1900) had ties to the British Isles, they happily accepted this situation.

When a British general asked for *voyageurs* to join an expedition to Sudan, Canadians were happy to step up. When Britain went to war against Boer settlers in South Africa, thousands of Canadians volunteered. When European countries engaged in an arms race before the First World War, Canadian politicians promised to stand by the Crown. Sir Wilfrid Laurier, then leader of the opposition, spoke for most Canadians in a speech to parliament. "When the call comes," he said, "our answer goes at once, and it goes in the classical language of the British answer to the call to duty: 'Ready, aye, ready.'"

Canadians were not so gung-ho when the Great War ended. The soldiers who had served on the Western Front between 1914 and 1918 endured horrors they could not have imagined when they started out. Their sacrifices were enormous: More than 66,000 Canadians died in that war.

And yet, what they achieved was remarkable.

They had left a colony and returned to a nation.

This is not strictly true, of course: Canada would not become an independent nation for many years. But never again would it go to war just because another country said so. Canadians had seen what war cost. They also had discovered what they were made of. The raw Canadian recruits who sailed to Britain when the war started, and survived the rigours of the Western front, became the brave, battle-hardened veterans who led the Allies to victory at the end.

THE MARCH OF HISTORY

Canadians sometimes forget the grim and glorious role that their soldiers, sailors, and aircrews have played in the world. They think of them as peace-keepers, not warriors. But they were warriors first.

They earned that name again in the Second World War. More than a million Canadian men and women wore military uniform overseas between 1939 and 1945. More than 44,000 were killed. They saw combat again in Korea, where 27,000 served, and more than 500 gave their lives. In the Persian Gulf, and, most recently, in Afghanistan, thousands more have fought and hundreds have died.

Of course, Canadians have played a vital role as peacekeepers, too. They have shown that it takes a soldier's discipline, courage, and presence of mind to stand between warring armies.

Canada's military men and women are among the best in the world. They are skilful, resourceful, determined, loyal, and willing to die for what they believe in. Those of us who live in the world's luckiest nation should never forget how much they are owed.

THE NILE BOATMEN

In 1884, a contingent of British soldiers was besieged by rebels in Sudan in North Africa. A British general, Garnet Wolsely, had seen Canadian voyageurs at work during the Red River uprising in 1870. Now he asked the Canadian government to send similar crews to guide a rescue mission up the Nile River. Nearly 400 expert boatmen volunteered. They included loggers from the Ottawa Valley and Native peoples from Canada's west. The boatmen did their job as guides. They were not asked to fight. The expedition failed when the rebels overwhelmed the British soldiers in Khartoum. The Nile voyageurs, however, were the first Canadians to take part in a foreign war.

Boers invade British colonies
October 12, 1899

RCR arrives in South Africa
November 29, 1899

Battle of Paardeberg Drift
February 18–27, 1900

AFRICAN GOLD RUSH

Two British colonies in southern Africa—Cape Colony and Natal—existed side by side with two formerly Dutch republics, the Orange Free State and Transvaal. Gold was discovered in Transvaal in the 1890s. The inhabitants—known as Boers—resented the flood of British colonists who poured into their republic to dig for gold. Relations between the British and the Boers grew strained. Finally, in October 1899, the Boers declared war on Britain.

THE CALL TO ARMS

Many English Canadians saw the Boer War as a great imperial adventure, but in Quebec the war was unpopular. Prime Minister Sir Wilfrid Laurier was opposed to Canadian participation. The pressure in favour of the war was so great, however, that he was forced to give in. The Canadian government raised, trained, and equipped a contingent made up entirely of volunteers. The British paid their wages.

The 2nd (Special Service) Battalion of the Royal Canadian Regiment of Infantry (RCR) stepped onto African soil on November 29, 1899. The Canadians fought as a distinct unit, under the command of a Canadian officer, Lieutenant-Colonel W.D. Otter. They saw action within a couple of months.

British troops wore pith helmets to provide protection from the sun, but the Canadians who followed the first contingent to Africa wore broad-brimmed Stetsons.

THE BATTLE OF PAARDEBERG DRIFT

Five thousand Boer troops under the command of General Piet Cronjé were trapped on the banks of the Modder River in the Orange Free State. British and Canadian forces, under the overall command of Field Marshal Lord Roberts, numbered 35,000. The battle was fierce, although the numbers favoured the attackers. The Boers dug defensive positions and fought hard.

The RCR was thrown into action on the morning of February 18, 1900. They came under heavy fire. The attack faltered and died before the British and Canadian forces came close to the Boer line. Roberts made up his mind to surround Cronjé's position and wait him out.

A week later, on the night of February 26, six companies of the RCR moved against the Boer positions. They were spotted when they came within about 100 metres of the enemy. There was an exchange of fire and the attackers were ordered to retire. For some reason, a company of Maritimers with the RCR never heard the order. They held their ground. When morning came, they found themselves on a hill overlooking the Boer trenches. They opened fire and the Boers surrendered.

The Canadians suffered 34 dead and about 100 wounded at Paardeberg Drift. It was the only set-piece battle (that is, a battle that was carefully planned ahead of time) they took part in.

A SOLDIER WRITES HOME

Douglas McPherson was one of the Canadians who took part in the Battle of Paardeberg Drift. In a letter home, he described the attack on the Boer trenches: "At eight we were firing at the place where we saw smoke, for no Boers were visible, although [we were] only 500 yards from their trenches. Here we lay all day with the bullets whistling and cracking all around us and no cover except the ant hills, which were far too scarce. Well, at about 5:30 p.m. we got the order to fix bayonets. . . . Well, we charged but we lay down where we were and when darkness came retired, but all night we were bringing in wounded. Next day, when the Boers left the position, I went all through their trenches and the place seemed to me to be impregnable to anything but artillery, and my only wonder was that more of us were not killed."

Above: Canadians at a first-aid station following the Battle of Paardeberg.
Opposite page: The 2nd Battalion RCR crosses the Modder River at Paardeberg Drift, February 1900.

THE QUEEN'S SCARF

Queen Victoria made eight scarves to honour Boer War heroes. Private Richard Rowland Thompson (below) of the RCR received one of them for his courageous actions at Paardeberg Drift. On February 18, he crawled onto the battlefield to aid a Canadian soldier who was bleeding heavily from a neck wound. Thompson stayed beside the man and tended his wound for seven hours under enemy fire. When enemy troops finally pulled back, both men were rescued.

BOER COMMANDOS

After the defeat at Paardeberg, the Boers avoided battles in the open. Instead, they fought a guerrilla war. Most of the Boer soldiers were farmers. They were excellent horsemen and hunters. They used these skills to harass, sabotage, and ambush British forces.

After the early battles, the Boer War became a series of hit-and-run attacks and skirmishes. Soldiers mounted on horses (cavalry) were well-suited to this kind of campaign.

THE END OF THE WAR

Lord Kitchener, who had been second-in-command to Roberts, took Roberts's place in November 1900. Kitchener pursued a harsh strategy to defeat the Boers. He destroyed their farms and forced their women and children into concentration camps. Conditions in the camps were terrible and thousands of the inmates died of hunger and disease. Many people in Britain and Canada turned against the war because of what they learned about the camps.

The Canadian government raised two contingents for service in South Africa in 1899 and 1900. More Canadians were recruited and equipped privately. Altogether, some 8,000 men enlisted, more than 200 died, and another 250 were wounded. The Boers surrendered on May 31, 1902.

REMEMBERING THE HORSES

Nearly every country in the world has monuments to its war dead, but a statue in Port Elizabeth, South Africa is different. It is a memorial to the thousands of horses that perished in the Boer War. It features a life-sized horse and a soldier kneeling to offer it a bucket of water. The inscription reads:

> "The greatness of a nation consists not so much in the number of its people or the extent of its territory as in the extent and justice of its compassion."

LORD STRATHCONA'S HORSE

Donald A. Smith, Lord Strathcona and Mount Royal, was part-owner of the Canadian Pacific Railway. He was one of the powerful men who helped to hammer home "the last spike" in the famous photograph.

Smith reckoned it was his patriotic duty to raise and pay for a new regiment for service in the Boer War. Smith asked Sam Steele (above), a superintendent in the North-West Mounted Police, to take command. Steele attracted many former Mounties and cowboys from Canada's west to Lord Strathcona's Horse. They arrived in South Africa in April 1900.

THE GREAT WAR

INCIDENT AT SARAJEVO

On Sunday, June 28, 1914, Gavrilo Princip, a member of the Black Hand, a Serbian secret society, murdered Archduke Franz Ferdinand, heir to the Austrian throne. The assassination was scarcely noticed in Ottawa: Canada's prime minister, Sir Robert Borden, made no mention of the event in his diary. Just the same, Ferdinand's death set off a chain of events that led to one of the most terrible wars in history. For Canada, the Great War would be an epic, blood-stained coming-of-age.

After Ferdinand's death, all Europe geared up for conflict. Austria declared war on Serbia. Russia mobilized its armies to protect the Serbs. Germany declared war on Russia. The Germans knew the French would side with the Russians and began to march through Belgium on their way to attack France. Britain, which had a secret understanding with France, sent Germany an ultimatum. Germany ignored the warning. When the ultimatum expired at midnight on August 4, Britain (and the British Empire) was at war.

There was no question that Britain spoke for Canada. A few days after war was declared, Borden sent a message to London, assuring Britain of Canada's support. Canadians, he wrote, were "united in a common resolve to put forth every effort and to make every sacrifice necessary to ensure the integrity and maintain the honour of the Empire."

Soldiers scuffle with a member of the Black Hand immediately after the murder of Archduke Ferdinand.

COLONEL SAM

Sam Hughes was a pompous bully. He had fought in the Boer War where he was brave but inclined to brag. He boasted that the British promised to award him the Victoria Cross, not just once but twice. He claimed that both times the promise was broken. The British eventually became fed up with him and sent him back to Canada.

Hughes distrusted full-time soldiers. He believed that an independent-minded volunteer was always more effective than a rule-bound regular soldier. He was not, perhaps, the best person to head the armed forces. But in 1911, he was a member of parliament when his party formed the government. Prime Minister Borden made him minister of militia and national defence.

Staff officers had made plans for war. Naturally, when war was declared, Hughes ignored their plans. He would raise the Canadian contingent *his* way. He sent personal telegrams to local militia units asking for volunteers. He appointed his friends to important positions. He refused to use the existing training camp at Petawawa in Ontario. Instead, he created a brand-new camp at Valcartier, Quebec. And he sent the Royal Canadian Regiment, Canada's most experienced soldiers, to take up guard duty in Bermuda. The RCR played no active role in the war until 1916.

FROM VALCARTIER . . .

Britain first asked Canada for 25,000 troops. Many more volunteers than that joined up. Most of them travelled to the new camp at Valcartier, Quebec.

The camp was just a vacant field at the beginning of August 1914. In a few frenzied weeks, contractors built roads, installed a water supply and drainage system, and constructed the world's biggest rifle range. (It was more than five kilometres long.) Rows of tents sprang up to shelter the new recruits. The first 8,000 men arrived in early September. Thousands more joined them before the end of the month. They were given very little training. They were lucky if they got uniforms and equipment. Sam Hughes was often seen in the chaos. He charged about the camp on horseback, shouting instructions and cursing everyone who got in his way.

Not everyone liked Hughes, but he did what he set out to do. More than 30,000 soldiers shipped out of Quebec City on October 3, 1914. Ten days later, thousands of Britons cheered their arrival in Plymouth, England. Both soldiers and civilians were exuberant. Almost everyone looked forward to a short, glorious war.

Tents and not much else await the new recruits arriving at Valcartier in late summer, 1914.

. . . TO SALISBURY PLAIN

The Canadians were sent to a camp on Salisbury Plain in Wiltshire, England. It was the beginning of one of the coldest and wettest winters in memory. The troops were miserable. Much of their equipment turned out to be inferior. Hughes had provided them with a "shield shovel" of his secretary's invention that was useless both as a shield and as a shovel. The soldiers' boots fell apart in the mud. Their Ross rifles, manufactured in Canada, were excellent for target practice but jammed in combat. Gradually, the Canadians discarded their second-rate gear for British equipment. They would have adopted the British gun, the Lee-Enfield, if Hughes had allowed it. Later, many Canadian soldiers would pick up British rifles they found on the battlefield.

Conditions on Salisbury Plain were so bad the second Canadian contingent was kept in Canada until the spring.

Volunteers continued to line up at recruiting stations in Canada through the spring of 1915. At first, the majority were British-born. Many came from Canada's west. Relatively few were French-speaking. News of the first battles encouraged new recruits to join up. This early enthusiasm gradually faded. By the end of 1915, most people understood that the war was not an adventure but a terrible, deadly grind.

Canadian soldiers splash through the mud and rain on Salisbury Plain in the winter of 1914–15.

REMEMBERING GALLIPOLI

"All over the Peninsula disease had become epidemic, until the clearing stations and the beaches were choked with sick. . . . By sickness and snipers' bullets we were losing thirty men a day. Nobody in the front-line trenches or on the shell-swept area behind ever expected to leave the Peninsula alive."

—Corporal Alonzo John Gallishaw,
Royal Newfoundland Regiment

THE FIRST FIVE HUNDRED

Newfoundland was a self-governing dominion with its own governor and prime minister. In August 1914, they formed the Newfoundland Patriotic Association to raise, equip, and finance a Newfoundland regiment. The "First Five Hundred" sailed for England in October.

The Newfoundlanders trained in England for ten months. In autumn 1915, they were sent to Gallipoli, in Turkey. Fierce battles had been fought there before their arrival. Anzac (Australian and New Zealand) troops had taken terrible losses in their attempts to defeat the Turkish troops. By the time the Newfoundland Regiment joined them, the two sides had fought to a standstill. The men suffered as much from disease as from the fighting. Eventually, the Newfoundland Regiment was sent to the Western Front, in Europe, early in 1916. Gallipoli was lost to the Turks.

The Newfoundland Regiment travelled to Gallipoli by way of Egypt. Some officers took the opportunity to visit the great pyramids at Giza, as this photograph shows.

IN FLANDERS FIELDS

"The artillery fire was constant, heavy and from all sorts of guns. . . . The men behaved magnificently; and the labour was terribly hard. In one 30 hours we fired 3,600 rounds: and at one time our brigade had only seven guns able to fire; two of these smoked at every joint and were too hot to touch with the unprotected hand. Throughout three nights they shelled us continuously; and the firing never ceased one consecutive minute, night or day; and yet the birds kept singing in the trees—what trees were not cut down by shells."

—Major John McCrae,
1st Brigade, Canadian Field Artillery
(McCrae is best known as the poet
who wrote "In Flanders Fields")

DISQUIET ON THE WESTERN FRONT

In August 1914, the British and French generals were full of confidence. They thought their cavalry and infantry would move quickly against the enemy and fight short, decisive battles. At first, it seemed that they were correct, but not in the way they expected. At Mons, Belgium, the British Expeditionary Force was pushed back by a much larger German army.

There was more movement, back and forth, in autumn 1914. It all slowed to a stop by the end of the year. Modern weapons, including machine guns and heavy artillery, made it easier to defend a position than to attack it. Armies were much larger than they had been in the past because volunteers, conscripts, and part-timers joined the ranks of professional soldiers. Both the Germans on one side, and the French and British on the other, were unable to advance. They built defences—bunkers, gun emplacements, and trenches—in a line that extended from Switzerland to the coast of Belgium. This line became the Western Front.

SECOND BATTLE OF YPRES

The Canadian Division reached France in February 1915. The men joined the British line to see what trench warfare was like. Then they marched to the town of Ypres, Belgium, to take up a position of their own.

The Germans had tried to break through the line in the First Battle of Ypres. They were pushed back and both sides dug in over the winter. The Canadians occupied a six-kilometre section of the line at the beginning of March. They were at the forward edge

of a bulge, or "salient," that poked into German-held territory. On their left was a French-Algerian division. On their right were two British divisions.

On April 22, with the wind in their favour, the Germans opened up thousands of cans of chlorine gas. Great clouds of the deadly mist rolled across the battlefield. The French contingent was devastated: the gas burned through the soldiers' noses and lips to sear their lungs. They gasped, choked, threw up, and collapsed. Hundreds of soldiers suffocated and died. The French sector dissolved but the Canadians held on.

The Germans advanced three kilometres into the gap—but then halted. That night, the Canadian 3rd Brigade was ordered to attack German forces in Kitchener's Wood near the village of St. Julien. The brigade cleared the woods but suffered heavy losses and pulled back. The following morning, April 23, the Canadians mounted two more attacks against the new German positions. These assaults gave the Allies time to bring reinforcements from the rear.

The Germans launched another gas attack on April 24. The Canadians held their position as clouds of gas rolled across the landscape. Both the 2nd and 3rd Brigades were engaged in desperate fighting at close quarters. The 3rd Brigade eventually withdrew 600 metres. The 2nd, although hard-pressed, stood firm. The Canadians were relieved on April 26.

More than 6,000 Canadians were killed or wounded in the Ypres Salient. By their courage and determination, they had prevented an Allied disaster.

The wind blows deadly chlorine gas across the battlefield. Gas masks were essential equipment, although they were uncomfortable to wear and a nuisance to carry. Later masks gave better protection.

IN THE TRENCHES

A trench was a ditch dug into the earth. The soldiers who took shelter in it were relatively safe. Only a direct hit by a mortar or artillery shell was likely to harm them. Trenches were easy to defend and dangerous to attack. Over the course of the war, trenches became more elaborate.

Usually there were three lines of trenches. The first was a "fire" trench that faced the enemy. The second "support" trench provided shelter if the first line came under fire. The third "reserve" line was home for the battalion headquarters along with cooks, signallers, and other specialists.

Strings and coils of barbed wire fronted the fire trenches. The wire was laid out in a pattern intended to funnel attackers towards the defenders' guns. The gap between the German and Allied lines was known as "no man's land." This dangerous wasteland ranged from 30 metres to more than a kilometre wide.

PLUM JAM

At best, the trenches were miserable. At worst, they were the scene of horror and suffering.

The trenches were often wet and sometimes flooded. They offered some protection from bullets but none from snow and rain. Later in the war, the soldiers shovelled holes in the sides to make cave-like dugouts. Timber posts and steel plates supported the walls and ceilings. Even the dugouts were damp, however, and infested by rats. There was no defence against lice. Feet that were always wet turned black with "trenchfoot." Any wound was likely to become infected.

During the day, the soldiers lay low. They kept an eye on enemy lines using mirrored periscopes. If they could, they made a hot meal or grabbed some sleep. The food wasn't great. They were given a kind of jam that, as one soldier wrote in a letter home, was "one of the mysteries of the war." The label said it was plum jam. The letter writer and his mates believed it was made from turnips. When they complained, their corporal replied sternly, "Boys, there's a war on."

The trenches gave almost no shelter from the elements. These men (below), some with the collars of their greatcoats pulled up around their necks, gather around a stove and smile for the camera. Inset above left: William Thurston Topham's painting shows a forward observation post on the Western Front.

AT NIGHT IN NO MAN'S LAND

The Canadians became skilled at conducting night raids. They blackened their faces and pulled on stocking caps and their oldest uniforms. They armed themselves with an assortment of weapons and crept out into no man's land under cover of darkness.

A successful raid was good for morale. In an early night raid on November 17, 1915, soldiers of the 1st Canadian Division took a dozen prisoners and inflicted 30 casualties on the enemy. Like every other action in this terrible war, however, night raids were costly. In a few months in the winter and spring of 1916, even though there were no major battles, British and Dominion forces lost 83,000 men. Night raids accounted for many of these losses.

Above: William Thurston Topham's painting, *Moonrise over Mametz Wood*, shows a portion of the Somme battlefield.

THE WAR GOES BADLY

The war was less than a year old but already the soldiers understood how bloody and brutal it would be. From Mons to Ypres, the British and their allies had seen what machine guns and modern artillery could do to exposed infantry. Yet the British high command still believed that bold action and courageous soldiers were all they needed to win the war.

In May 1915, Lieutenant-General Sir Edwin Alderson, a British officer who commanded the 1st Canadian Division, ordered the 2nd and 3rd Brigades to take K5, a hill near the hamlet of Festubert. The Canadians attacked the position repeatedly over a period of five days. In the end, they gained 600 metres of ground and lost 2,468 killed and wounded. A month later, at Givenchy, the Canadians fought another brave but futile battle and lost 366 men.

Little had changed a year later. In April 1916, the 2nd Division was sent to defend a half-dozen craters on the line at St. Eloi. A German assault forced the Canadians to give up all but a small section of the muddy landscape at a cost of more than 1,300 men. The Allies were taking fearful losses on the Western Front.

SISTERS OF MERCY

A dozen doctors and more than 100 nurses of the Canadian Army Medical Service sailed with the soldiers from Quebec City in October 1914. By late November, they had established their first hospital—Stationary Hospital No. 2—in the resort town of Le Touquet on the French coast. In spring 1915, some of the Canadians who had been gassed or wounded at Ypres were cared for by friendly nurses—they were called "nursing sisters"—from home.

Above: Laura Gamble (on the right).
Below: Canadian soldiers carry a wounded comrade to the aid station at Passchendaele, November 1917.

British nurses formed an auxiliary service but the Canadians were part of the army. Laura Gamble was a nurse at Toronto General Hospital before the war. She went on to serve in England, France, and Greece. She was one of more than 2,800 Canadian nursing sisters who served overseas in the First World War.

When a soldier was wounded, he was taken to a regimental aid post, then to a casualty clearing station. Doctors there administered first aid. Within a day or so, if he needed further attention, the soldier was moved to a military hospital. Finally, if his condition was bad enough, he might be sent to "dear old Blighty," a slang name for England. Some weary soldiers were glad to get a wound—a "blighty"—that was just bad enough to need treatment on the peaceful side of the English Channel.

Sir Julian Byng

OFFICERS AND MEN

Sam Hughes wanted to command the Canadian contingent himself but the British would not let him. Instead, they put forward a British general, Sir Edwin Alderson, who had commanded Canadian troops in the Boer War. Alderson immediately came into conflict with Hughes. He fired some of Hughes's officers. He also criticized the Ross rifle. After the disaster at St. Eloi, Hughes pressed for Alderson to be fired. He got his way. Alderson was replaced by another British general, Sir Julian Byng.

The 1st Canadian Division was joined in France by the 2nd Division in September 1915. The 3rd Division followed in December 1915. Finally, the 4th Division, formed early in 1916, completed the Canadian contribution to Allied land forces in Europe.

The four divisions were commanded by Canadians after 1915. The 1st Division was led by Arthur Currie, who had been a businessman in peacetime; the 2nd Division by R.E.W. Turner, who had won a Victoria Cross in the Boer War; the 3rd Division by Malcolm Smith Mercer, who would be killed at Mount Sorrel; the 4th by David Watson, a friend of Hughes.

Sir Arthur Currie

Byng turned out to be a popular leader. Canadian troops started calling themselves the "Byng Boys." Beginning in fall 1916, under Byng's command, the Canadians achieved some notable victories. In 1917, Byng was promoted, and Arthur Currie became commander of the Canadian Corps. Currie would lead Canadian troops to their greatest triumphs in the last year of the war.

"Let his heart a thousandfold Take the field again!"

ARE YOU ONE OF KITCHENER'S OWN?

NOW RECRUITING UNDER Lt.Col. F. M. McROBIE, HIGH SCHOOL BARRACKS, 197 PEEL STREET, MONTREAL.

THE CALL

"I was in the [college] library in 1915, studying a Latin poet, and all of a sudden I thought: 'War can't be this bad.' So I walked out and enlisted."
—Lester Pearson, future prime minister of Canada, recalling his service in the First World War

JEREMIAH JONES

Black Canadians who tried to enlist in the army often were refused by racist recruiters who told them it was a "white man's war." One who succeeded was a man known as a "friendly giant," Jeremiah Jones from Truro, Nova Scotia.

Jones was a private serving with the RCR at Vimy Ridge. He took an enemy machine-gun post single-handedly. "I threw a hand bomb right into the nest and killed about seven of them," he explained later. "I was going to throw another bomb, when they threw up their arms and called for mercy."

THE PRINCESS PATS

Hamilton Gault, a wealthy Montreal businessman, decided to raise a regiment of his own in 1914. He asked the governor general, the Duke of Connaught, for permission to ask his daughter, Princess Patricia, if she would be the regiment's colonel-in-chief. She agreed and sewed the regiment's colours (that is, its ceremonial flag).

Three thousand men showed up at Ottawa's Lansdowne Park to volunteer for the new regiment. Roughly 1,000 were chosen. Almost all of them were British veterans of earlier wars. They became known as the "Old Originals."

NATIVE VOLUNTEERS

More than 4,000 Native Canadians volunteered for service in the Great War. Some reserves gave up nearly all their young men to the armed forces. The Iroquois Six Nations, near Brantford, Ontario, provided more than 300 soldiers for the 107th Battalion, a Winnipeg unit. Some Native recruits used their experience as hunters and outdoorsmen to deadly effect. Francis Pegahmagabow (above), a Parry Island Ojibwa, saw action with the 1st Division from Ypres to Amiens. Henry Louis Norwest, a Métis marksman from Fort Saskatchewan, Alberta, was credited with 115 fatal shots. Both were decorated for their achievements. Two sons of Six Nations Cayuga Chief Alexander George Smith, Charles and Alexander Jr., served overseas with the 1st Division. They, too, were awarded the Military Cross for exceptional bravery.

Left: Princess Patricia of Connaught made the regiment's colours herself.

MOUNT SORREL

In June 1916, soldiers of the newly arrived 3rd Division came under fire at Mount Sorrel. The German bombardment was the heaviest yet endured by Canadian troops: whole trenches were blown away, and the Canadians were forced to pull back. They mounted a counteroffensive the next day. It failed. German forces occupied Mount Sorrel and two nearby hills. The hills were given numbers rather than names: Hills 61 and 62. Sir Julian Byng undertook to take the positions back. He planned the attack carefully, and the troops rehearsed their roles. Early in the morning on June 13, the Canadians advanced behind a heavy artillery barrage. They dislodged the Germans but the cost was dreadful: 8,430 killed, wounded, or missing.

THE BIG PUSH

St. Eloi and Mount Sorrel were diversions meant to fool the Germans. The British planned a major offensive far away, on the Somme River, in which they hoped to break through the German lines. It began with a bloodbath. On a single day, July 1, 1916, 57,500 Allied troops were killed, wounded, or went missing. The Newfoundland Regiment, in action for the first time since Gallipoli, was among the many units decimated that day. The Newfoundlanders were ordered to advance

against German trenches at Beaumont Hamel. Not a single man made it to the German line. Only 68 escaped without a scar; 684 were either killed or wounded.

Canadians were drawn into the "Big Push" beginning in August when elements of the Canadian Corps met the enemy at Courcelette. In September, they were sent to take the "Sugar Factory," a nearby German bastion. The Canadians finally were using new tactics and weapons. A half-dozen tanks accompanied the troops assaulting the Sugar Factory. They all broke down—tanks were still clumsy and new—but their appearance scared the enemy. Troops followed their own rolling barrage of artillery fire that softened the defences in front of them. The infantry no longer advanced in an endless line. Instead, they formed small units—platoons—that could respond to conditions as they encountered them. These changes worked: the Canadians took their objectives.

The Somme offensive ended in November 1916. It had been a disastrous year for the Allies. But the Canadians now were thoroughly battle-hardened, a force to be reckoned with.

Relief troops move forward while their weary comrades head for the rear on the Somme in 1916.

TRIUMPH AT VIMY RIDGE

The British launched another offensive in spring 1917, this one on the Arras front in Belgium. The four divisions of the Canadian Corps were ordered to take Vimy Ridge. The Germans had occupied the area since the beginning of the war. Earlier attempts by the French and British to dislodge them had failed. But the Allies, and especially Byng, had finally learned how to come out ahead in this dreadful war.

Byng's plans were meticulous. The troops studied scale models of their objectives and rehearsed their assignments ahead of time. They stockpiled arms and supplies in trenches behind them. They dug tunnels under the German lines. When the time came, they set off mines in the tunnels to destroy the German defences. The artillery bombardment that preceded the attack was long and devastating. It was directed by a 30-year-old lieutenant-colonel, Andrew McNaughton (inset below), of the Canadian Field Artillery.

Inset below, right:
A naval gun joins
the barrage at
Vimy Ridge.

The first wave of Canadian infantry—15,000 men—went over the top of the trenches at 5:30 a.m. on April 9. Another two waves followed. After a day of ferocious fighting, the Canadians took control of the principal height of land, Hill 145. Machine guns on a second hill, which the Canadians called the "Pimple," slowed the Canadian advance. Not until April 12 was the Pimple taken.

The Battle of Vimy Ridge was the most significant advance that the Allies had made. The Canadians took about 4,000 prisoners. They lost nearly as many of their own: 3,598 killed or lost in action.

CANADA'S COMING OF AGE

Byng was promoted in June 1917. His place as corps commander was taken by Arthur (now Sir Arthur) Currie. By this stage of the war, so many men had been lost that all units were shorthanded. The British wanted the Canadian divisions to be used as the British wished. Currie argued strongly against the proposal. He said the Canadians would be effective only if they fought together. Canada's large contribution to the war had given its leaders a voice in the Empire. The British Secretary of State for War sadly informed Field Marshal Haig that Canada's wishes had to be respected. "I am afraid . . . we must look upon them in the light in which they wish to be looked upon rather than the light in which we should wish to do so. They look upon themselves, not as part and parcel of the English Army but as allies beside us."

PASSCHENDAELE

After a French offensive failed in April 1917, a number of units in the French army, worn out by the war in the trenches, rebelled against their commanders. The mutinies were kept secret from the public.

Field Marshal Haig believed, mistakenly, that German troops, too, were ready to quit. He decided to launch another British offensive in Belgium. He intended to drive towards the coast and shut down the ports from which German U-boats were operating. His target was the line beyond Ypres at Passchendaele.

British and Anzac troops launched repeated attacks on the German defences beginning in July 1917. Heavy shelling and endless rain turned the battlefield into a waterlogged wasteland. The Canadian Corps took over from the British in late October. Men who remembered the Flanders landscape from earlier campaigns were amazed by the change. Once poppies covered the fields. Now there was nothing.

Currie at first refused the order to attack. The mud made movement difficult. Big guns were stuck in the ooze. Roads, buildings, whole forests—any landmarks that would keep men from getting lost—had disappeared. He estimated that he would lose 16,000 troops in the operation. Haig overruled his objections. Currie then made the best plans he could. He demanded artillery to replace the guns that had been lost in earlier battles. His engineers built new supply and communications lines.

The 3rd and 4th Divisions engaged the enemy on October 26. Conditions were dreadful. The men were already weighed down by their rifles and supplies. The mud clinging to their clothes made their burden heavier. They were under constant fire. Some actually drowned in the water-filled craters. After five days, the troops had fought their way to within a few hundred metres of the village of Passchendaele. Currie pulled the first two divisions out, took time to reposition his artillery, and then sent fresh troops from the 1st and 2nd Divisions forward on November 6.

The final advance on Passchendaele achieved its objective. The Canadians lost 15,654 men, killed, wounded, and missing in action. Currie's estimate had been cruelly accurate.

THE BATTLE FOR AIR SUPREMACY

Hardly anyone guessed in 1914 that airplanes would play a significant part in the war. There was no Canadian air force. The British Royal Flying Corps (RFC) consisted of just four squadrons of airplanes. Mostly, the planes were used for observation. By 1916, however, it was apparent that the airplane would become a powerful weapon.

Canadians seemed to have an instinct for the air war. Approximately 7,000 Canadians served with the RFC. Perhaps as many as one-third of British aircrews were Canadian. Their occupation was extremely dangerous. Their planes were primitive and prone to failure: for much of the war, the German planes were faster and more robust. In the five days before the Battle of Vimy Ridge, the RFC lost 75 planes in action and another 56 to accidents. But gradually, the Allies' aircraft improved, and so did their pilots.

The Canadian government set out to create a Canadian Air Force in 1918. When the war ended in November, however, the government changed its mind.

ROY BROWN AND THE RED BARON

Manfred von Richthofen really was a baron. He learned to fly after the war started, in 1915, and soon showed that he was a brilliant pilot. He led Jasta 11, a German unit that became known as the Flying Circus. The planes in the Flying Circus were painted in bright colours (Richthofen's was red) so they could be easily identified. Between October 1916 and April 1918, Jasta 11 shot down 644 Allied planes while losing only 52.

Arthur Roy Brown was the son of a businessman in Carleton Place, Ontario. He learned to fly at a private school in Ohio and joined the RFC in 1916. As flight commander, Brown took pride in looking after his pilots. On their first missions, Brown would fly above them, ready to intervene if they got into trouble.

On April 21, 1918, one of the pilots in Brown's unit was in serious trouble. Wilfrid "Wop" May was flying low over the Somme when the Red Baron swooped down on his tail with guns blazing. Brown swooped down on them both. Richthofen's plane went into a tailspin and crashed. There is some evidence that Richthofen was killed by a bullet fired from the ground but the RFC gave Brown credit for the kill. Brown did not relish the recognition. He said the death of the great German pilot saddened him.

ACE WAR ACE

Billy Bishop volunteered to serve with the Mississauga Horse at the beginning of the war. He was training in England one day—it was raining and he was up to his knees in mud—when he looked up and saw an airplane. He thought to himself that he would be a much happier man above the clouds than he was below them. He asked to be transferred to the RFC.

He flew his first missions against the enemy in 1917. He demonstrated his skill from the start and soon his exploits became legendary. He earned almost every medal that was available, including the Victoria Cross, which was given to him for a single-handed attack on an enemy airfield. His 72 victories made him the most famous Canadian to fight in the war.

F.H. Varley portrayed air combat in his sketch *The Young Man's Element, the Air*, in 1917.

Canadian troops pick their way through the rubble of Cambrai in October 1918.

THE UNITED STATES JOINS IN

For much of the war, German U-boats attacked neutral ships on the high seas. The United States was neutral, but its ships were not. Britain depended upon supplies from the United States to support the war effort. In summer 1916, Germany, hoping to keep the Americans from entering the war, stopped unrestricted U-boat attacks. Early in 1917, however, Germany decided that it had to attack all shipping bound for Europe to win the war. Its U-boats quickly sank seven American merchant ships. In April, the United States declared war. The first American troops arrived in France in June 1917.

The European armies were exhausted. The entry of a powerful nation that had been largely untouched by war would prove to be decisive. The German high command tried to end the war before the Americans had landed in force by launching a major offensive in March 1918. The offensive failed after huge gains were made. By June 1918, tens of thousands of American troops had arrived—enough to make a difference.

AMIENS

After four years of fighting, the British and their allies finally had the weapons and tactics needed to end trench warfare. Troops were more mobile. Tanks were more reliable. And the Canadians, especially, had become resilient and aggressive warriors.

Their reputation in battle was fearsome. When Haig planned a major offensive at Amiens, France, in August 1918, the Canadians were taken to the front in secret. No Canadians were used in early raids to explore the German line in case one was taken prisoner. If the Germans had discovered a Canadian on the line, they would have known a major attack was coming.

Four hundred and seventy tanks were used in the assault that began on August 8. British, Australian, and Canadian divisions made their biggest single-day advance since the first year of the war. The Canadians advanced farthest of all—about 13 kilometres. Erich Ludendorff, one of the officers in charge of the German war effort, declared that it was a "black day" for the German army. He told the Kaiser (the German head of state) that the war was lost.

THE HUNDRED DAYS

Amiens was a turning point. In the 100 days that followed, the Canadian Corps formed the spearhead of the Allied attack. Under Sir Arthur Currie's brilliant leadership, the Canadians were involved in one important victory after another. From the end of August through September, they attacked the German Hindenburg Line, a series of defences in France that had to be broken, one by one, until they reached the Canal du Nord. In October, they took Cambrai. From Cambrai, they marched to Valenciennes, and then finally to Mons, Belgium.

The going was not easy: one-fifth of all Canadian casualties occurred in the last few months of the war. But the enemy was on the run at last. One soldier observed, as his battalion closed in on Valenciennes, that the fighting was no longer heavy and the Germans "were surrendering in droves. . . . We knew that the enemy was practically breaking up."

WITH SABRES DRAWN

Sixty years had passed since the disastrous Charge of the Light Brigade at Balaclava in the Crimean War. Still, there were generals who believed that cavalry had a part to play in warfare. On March 30, 1918, a squadron of the Lord Strathcona's Horse, led by Lieutenant G.M. Flowerdew (above), was ordered to attack German infantry at Moreuil Wood, near Amiens. The Canadians were cut to pieces. Flowerdew, fatally wounded in the attack, was awarded the Victoria Cross posthumously.

THE WAR ARTISTS

An energetic Canadian businessman, Max Aitken, moved to London where he became Lord Beaverbrook, a member of the House of Lords. In 1916, he established the Canadian War Memorials Fund. This was the first government body created by an Allied country that paid artists to paint what they saw of the war.

The first painter hired under the program was an Englishman, Richard Jack. His paintings represented imagined battle scenes and focused on the heroism of individual soldiers. A.Y. Jackson, who later would become one of the founding members of the Group of Seven, was commissioned in August 1917. Five more Canadians soon followed and were sent to France: J.W. Morrice, Maurice Cullen, Charles Simpson, J.W. Beatty, and F.H. Varley. Varley—another member of the Group of Seven—visited the Western Front in the final months of the war. The experience had a profound impact on him. His paintings, unlike Jack's, convey the horror, desolation, and pointlessness of the war.

"You in Canada . . . cannot realize at all what war is like. You must see it and live it. You must see the turned-up graves, see the dead on the field, freakishly mutilated— headless, legless, stomachless, a perfect body and a passive face and a broken empty skull—see your own countrymen, unidentified, thrown into a cart, their coats thrown over them, boys digging a grave in a land of yellow slimy mud and green pools of water under a weeping sky."

—F.H. Varley, in a letter home

Varley's grim painting, *For What?*, emphasized the horror of the war.

THE END, AT LAST

For weeks, the soldiers at the front had heard rumours that the war would soon end. Currie was ordered to keep fighting just the same. The German army continued bitterly to resist the Allied assault. The Canadians fought their way into Mons, Belgium, on the morning of November 11, 1918.

Mons was where the British Empire's war had started. In 1914, the British had been forced to retreat from Mons by the advancing German army. It was a fitting place to learn that an armistice had been signed at last.

The Canadians in the combat zone were glad it was over. They felt relief, and sadness for their fallen comrades, rather than jubilation. A private serving with the Canadian Corps, Floyd White, wrote a letter to his mother on the day after the armistice was declared. "I don't mind telling you now," he wrote, "that there was a time, not very long ago that I had given up all hope of ever seeing 53 New Street again."

THE CANADIAN ACHIEVEMENT

The hundred days that led up to the signing of the armistice were incredible days for Canada. The four divisions of the Canadian Corps were only a small part of the armies that fought for the Allies. Their numbers were modest but their contribution was huge. They led the way in the final advance through France and Belgium. Their courage, combined with Currie's brilliance, played a significant role in the Allied triumph.

When the war began, Great Britain was the centre of a vast, worldwide empire in which Canada occupied a tiny position. The British government did not even consult Canada before declaring war. By the end of the war, Canada was much closer to acting as an independent nation. And the British Empire was in decline.

THE COST

More than 650,000 men and a handful of women served in Canada's and Newfoundland's forces in the Great War. Of these, more than 66,000 sacrificed their lives and another 170,000 were wounded. The loss of so many young men and women—many barely out of their teens—would be felt keenly for years to come.

Opposite, top and bottom: Canadian soldiers in the streets of Mons, Belgium, on the morning of November 11, 1918. The Canadians were relieved and tired when they got news that the war was over at last. These soldiers look like they're ready to go home.

Above: Jubilant Canadians pour into the streets of Toronto (top, left and right), Calgary (middle), and Vancouver (bottom) to celebrate the armistice.

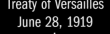

Treaty of Versailles
June 28, 1919

Mussolini takes power in Italy
October 28, 1922

Hitler takes power in Germany
January 30, 1933

THE RISE OF FASCISM

VERSAILLES

The Great War had started in confusion. There is no doubt, however, that Germany was the aggressor. The war ended quite simply: America entered the war and the Allies inflicted a series of decisive defeats on the German army. Weeks after Ludendorff told the Kaiser that his army had no hope of winning, the Germans finally, in October 1918, initiated peace negotiations.

The war had been devastating to the countries on whose territory it was fought. France and Belgium were especially badly damaged. While the German people had suffered, too, the physical damage on German territory was comparatively slight. Later, some Germans, including Ludendorff, who conveniently "forgot" his own words to his leader, would make much of the fact that Germany had not fallen to the Allies. They would argue, falsely, that their politicians had given up too soon. They also would complain that the terms of the peace treaty were too harsh.

The peace agreement was worked out at Versailles, France, in 1919. The Allies, especially England and France, were worried that Germany could rise again as a military power. The French also wanted to make their enemy pay for what it had done. The treaty required Germany to hand over its main industrial region to France for 15 years. It lost territory in Europe and colonies in Africa and the Pacific. It had to disband almost all its armed forces. And it was made to pay reparations to the victorious nations. These penalties made Germany weaker, as they were intended to do. They also meant that Germany would go through a period of political unrest and financial instability.

Benito Mussolini and Adolf Hitler in Munich, 1940.

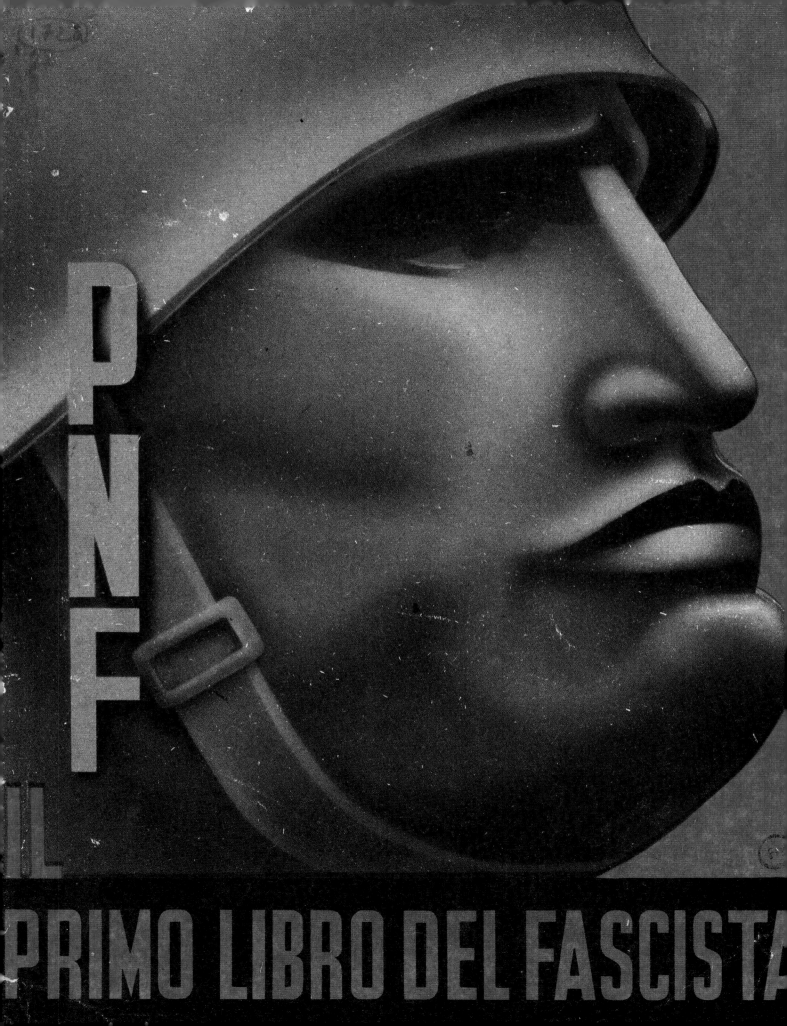

P N F

IL

PRIMO LIBRO DEL FASCISTA

HITLER AND MUSSOLINI

Italy had been a poor country before the war. It had fought against Germany, but it gained very little from the Treaty of Versailles. Returning soldiers could find no jobs as civilians. The government, which was corrupt, was unable to solve these problems. A new political movement emerged from the chaos. Benito Mussolini created his Fascist Party in 1919. The party emphasized an aggressive foreign policy and opposition to communism. A private militia, the Black Shirts, terrorized opponents. In 1922, Mussolini staged a coup d'état: He became prime minister of Italy.

Germany experienced similar problems. The government was unstable. The economy was in ruins. Adolf Hitler started a radical political movement similar to Mussolini's. Hitler's Brown Shirts attacked his rivals. They also targeted Jews. Hitler became chancellor of Germany in 1933. He immediately began undoing the Versailles treaty.

He built up Germany's armed forces. He sent troops into the territory that had been given to the French. His foreign policy became increasingly aggressive. He spoke of expanding Germany's borders to create more "living space" for the Germanic peoples. Although many of the world's leaders were reluctant to face it, Hitler was preparing for war.

Fascism was an ugly political movement in Italy. It was worse than this in Germany. Germany had greater industrial resources and a powerful military tradition. In Adolf Hitler, it had a leader who was as ruthless as he was immoral. Hitler and his Nazi Party celebrated violence and the rule of the strong over the weak. And he preached a racial hatred that would lead to the most horrifying crime committed by a modern state: the deliberate murder of more than six million Jews.

ADOLF HITLER, PATRIOT

In June 1937, after meetings in London with British and Commonwealth politicians, Canada's prime minister, William Lyon Mackenzie King (above), travelled to Berlin and met with Adolf Hitler. He was reassured by the encounter. King later described the chancellor as "a genuine patriot." His face, wrote King in his diary, "is not that of a fiery, over-strained nature, but of a calm, passive man, deeply and thoughtfully in earnest." King, to his credit, warned Hitler that if any part of the British Empire were threatened by an act of aggression, Canada would join with Britain to defend its freedom. Hitler paid no attention to the warning. King, however, was satisfied that he had done his bit for world peace.

Opposite page: Mussolini was pictured in Italian magazines as a kind of superman.

COMMUNISM, FASCISM, AND DEMOCRACY

Two radical political ideas attracted followers in the troubled years after the end of the Great War. The fascists in Italy and Germany believed that the state had to be led by an all-powerful leader supported by a strong military. Fascists did not tolerate any kind of dissent. They believed that a woman's place was in the home and that the population must be racially "pure."

The communist government in Soviet Russia was based on ideas first expressed by the German economist, Karl Marx. In theory, under communism, everyone shared equally in the wealth of the nation. Communists were opposed to the "capitalists" who owned or made money from factories and banks. They called on working men and women to rise up against them. In practice, the Soviet Union, like fascist Germany, was a dictatorship that denied most freedoms to its people.

Communist and fascist leaders used their political beliefs to justify aggression against neighbouring countries. Much recent history, from the Spanish Civil War to the end of the 20th century, is about the contest between Western democracies and fascist and communist dictatorships.

Opposite page: Thousands of volunteers from Europe, the United States, and Canada joined the International Brigades in Spain.

BETHUNE IN SPAIN

Norman Bethune (below) was a brilliant, difficult, and driven man. He trained as a surgeon and served in the Great War as a stretcher bearer. He was an innovator who tried constantly to improve the practice of medicine. He also had a strong social conscience: he was keenly aware that poor and disadvantaged people suffered more from disease than those who were better off. After a visit to the Soviet Union in 1935, he became a communist.

In 1936, Bethune went to Spain, which was then engaged in a civil war. He took with him a new technique for delivering blood transfusions to men and women wounded in battle. His mobile service, the first of its kind, operated as close as possible to the front lines. It saved many lives.

Bethune's temper and mood swings made him difficult to work with. By summer 1937, his relationship with the Spanish doctors, who were his colleagues, was strained. Bethune returned to Canada for a period. He then joined the communist Chinese in their battle with the nationalists and Japanese. He is famous in China, where he is regarded as a hero of the Communist Revolution. He died of blood poisoning in 1939.

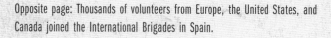

THE MAC-PAPS

In 1936, a democratically elected socialist government took power in Spain. The Spanish army, led by General Francisco Franco, opposed it. Franco tried to overthrow the government. When his coup attempt failed, he led the armed forces against the civilian authorities. A bloody civil war ensued.

The government forces, the Republicans, were supported by Soviet Russia. Franco, whose army and backers were called Nationalists, was supported by Italy and Germany. Thousands of volunteers from Europe and North America joined the International Brigades that fought for the Republicans in Spain.

About 1,300 Canadians formed the Mackenzie-Papineau Battalion in 1937 to fight with the Republicans. They were involved in a number of battles and almost half the Canadian volunteers were killed.

The armed forces led by Franco, with warplanes flown by German and Italian pilots, vanquished the Republicans. German planes dropping bombs on Spanish cities killed thousands of civilians. It was an indication of the role air power would play in future wars. Franco's fascist dictatorship governed Spain until his death in 1975.

EMPIRE OF THE EAST

Japan was a monarchy headed by an emperor. Like Germany and Italy, Japan also went through hard times after the Great War. The Emperor encouraged the armed forces to take over the government. He planned to solve Japan's economic problems by occupying other countries in the Far East.

In 1937, Japan invaded China. In the next few years, while Germany and Italy tried to carve up Europe, Japan set its sights on the Philippines, Indochina, Manchuria, Dutch East Indies, Malaysia, and Hong Kong. In 1940, Germany, Italy, and Japan signed a non-aggression pact. They became known as the Axis Alliance.

Opposite: British Prime Minister Neville Chamberlain clutches the agreement signed with Hitler in 1938.

THE GATHERING STORM

Some Canadians sympathized with the fascists. Few were bothered by the oppression of Europe's minorities. When Jewish families fled Germany in the 1930s, the Canadian government made it difficult for them to settle in Canada. (There were people who hated Jews in Canada, too). Prime Minister Mackenzie King was not blind to the threat posed by Germany. He knew that war was possible. He did not know—no one did—that the Nazis would commit horrifying atrocities in the years ahead. King's greatest fear was a practical one: that a war in Europe would divide Canada. He knew that many Canadians, especially in Quebec, were opposed to Canadian participation in another European war. So it is not surprising that King supported the British policy of appeasement.

In the late 1930s, Hitler moved to expand German territory in Europe. British Prime Minister Neville Chamberlain's response was cautious. Britain did nothing when Germany swept into Austria in March 1938. That summer, Hitler put pressure on the Czech government to give up the Sudetenland, a part of Czechoslovakia whose population mainly spoke German. Britain and France became involved in the negotiations to head off a German invasion. In September, Chamberlain met Hitler in Munich. Hitler agreed to take only part of Czechoslovakia. Chamberlain triumphantly declared that there would be "peace in our time." King—and most Canadians—applauded him.

In March 1939, Germany seized the rest of Czechoslovakia. In August, Germany and Soviet Russia agreed that neither country would attack the other. The pact was a surprise because Hitler claimed to be anti-communist. The agreement meant that Hitler could fight a war in Europe and not worry about Russia attacking him from behind. On September 1, German troops, led by the tanks of its armoured divisions, rolled into Poland. Hitler ignored a British demand that he pull back the tanks. On September 3, King George VI declared that Britain was at war with Germany.

ONE WEEK LATER . . .

In 1914, Britain's declaration of war had been Canada's also. In 1939, Canada was not at war until the Canadian parliament said it was. On Saturday, September 9, all but a handful of Canadian parliamentarians supported the call to arms. Even the MPs from Quebec voted in favour of the resolution. The governor general communicated Canada's decision to Britain. The next day, the King declared war on behalf of Canada.

Canada declares war
September 10, 1939

Evacuation of Dunkirk
May 26–June 4, 1940

France surrenders
June 25, 1940

Fall of Hong Kong
December 25, 1941

Dieppe raid
August 19, 1942

Canadians land on Sicily
July 10, 1943

| Battle of Ortona | Invasion of France begins | Germany surrenders |
| December 20–28, 1943 | June 6, 1944 | May 5, 1945 |

THE WORLD AT WAR

READY, NOT READY

There was a strange pause in the war—it became known as the Phony War or *drôle de guerre*—after Germany occupied Poland. War had been declared, territory had been seized, but there was a freeze on hostilities. It was not a total stoppage: German U-boats feasted on Allied shipping in the Atlantic Ocean. But Europe was oddly calm while diplomats tried to find a way to make peace behind the scenes.

Canada had virtually disarmed after the end of the Great War. The country had begun to prepare again for war in the late 1930s. The government had approved the creation of an air reserve. Some planes had been purchased for the Royal Canadian Air Force (RCAF). A handful of destroyers and mine-sweepers were added to the navy's fleet. But there actually were *fewer* trained members of the militia in 1939 than there had been in 1913. By no stretch of the imagination was Canada ready for what was to come.

Mackenzie King announced that Canada would raise two divisions for the war. The 1st Division would be sent overseas as soon as possible. The 2nd Division would be stationed at home. It would be sent to Britain only if it was needed. King hoped it wouldn't be. The end of the Phony War ended King's hoped-for short war.

Thousands of airmen were trained in Canada under the British Commonwealth Air Training Plan.

PILOT PROJECT

In December 1939, Canada agreed with the British to establish a program for training aircrews. Originally, it was intended that 20,000 recruits would be trained each year at 120 airfields across Canada. Most of the airfields were civilian. Many of them were operated by flying clubs. Private contractors maintained and repaired the aircraft. Over the course of the war, the British Commonwealth Air Training Plan trained more than 130,000 aircrew, including about 50,000 pilots, from Britain, Canada, Australia, and New Zealand. The BCATP made a major contribution to the war effort.

Cornells, propeller-driven aircraft, were used to train new pilots.

BLITZKRIEG!

Anyone who thought that this war would be like the First World War was in for a surprise. Germany's Luftwaffe (air force) and panzer (armoured) divisions blew their way through barbed wire, bunkers, and other fixed defences with terrifying speed. In April 1940, Hitler struck Denmark and Norway. In May, his blitzkrieg, or "lightning war," tore through the Netherlands, Belgium, and northern France. By June 4, the last remnants of the British Expeditionary Force had retreated across the English Channel by way of Dunkirk, France. Soon after, France surrendered.

Canada had entered the war ill-prepared and without enthusiasm. After the shocking collapse of France, however, Canadians suddenly realized they were Britain's chief remaining ally. Mackenzie King's government had to revise its plans.

All elements of the 1st Canadian Division had arrived in England by February 1940. In May, King announced that the 2nd Division would follow it overseas to make up the 1st Canadian Corps. A third division would be recruited immediately. Eventually, Canadians would send five divisions to Europe, making two corps—and a single army.

The commander of the Canadian Corps, eventually General Officer Commanding the Canadian Army, was Andrew McNaughton. He was the artillery officer who had proven his skill at Vimy Ridge in 1917. The Canadians would fight as a national unit throughout the war. Their senior officers reported to British and, later, Allied commanders.

THE "ENEMIES" WITHIN

Camillien Houde was the mayor of Montreal in 1940. He was a shrewd and popular Quebec nationalist. He had surprised some English Canadians in 1939 by graciously welcoming the King and Queen to the city. (Many people in Quebec wanted to cut all traditional ties to Britain.) But he also understood that many of his constituents were opposed to the war. When the federal government announced its intention to register all Canadian men in what was plainly preparation for possible conscription (compulsory miltary service), Houde denounced the law. He was promptly interned (imprisoned) as a subversive.

Houde was held in an internment camp in Petawawa, Ontario. He showed his political skills again by being elected mayor of the camp by his fellow inmates. When he was released in August 1944, thousands of Montrealers greeted him as a hero. He was re-elected mayor of the city in the election that followed.

Houde turned internment to his advantage. Others were less fortunate. Hundreds of Canadians whose families had come from Japan were interned after the attack on Pearl Harbor, Hawaii in 1941. Thousands more were forced to move away from the west coast. Few, if any, of the people affected sympathized with Japanese aggression. Just the same, they lost their freedom, their jobs, their homes, and their possessions. The federal government apologized to these Canadians and their descendants in 1988.

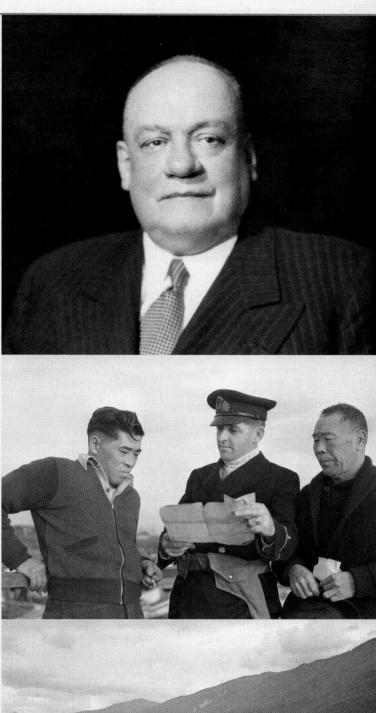

Among the "subversives" who were interned during the war was Montreal's mayor, Camillien Houde (top). Thousands of Japanese Canadians, such as these west-coast fishermen (middle), were sent to live in internment camps in the British Columbia interior (bottom).

THE FALL OF HONG KONG

Hong Kong, the great port and trading centre on China's coast, was a British colony. In autumn 1941, the Allies suspected that Japan was planning an attack. Canada was asked to send troops to help defend the city. Two Canadian battalions embarked on the SS *Awatea* in October 1941. They were from two regiments: the Winnipeg Grenadiers and the Royal Rifles of Canada. Neither battalion was properly trained or fully equipped when it arrived in Hong Kong in November.

On December 8, 1941, the day after they had attacked the American naval base at Pearl Harbor, the Japanese invaded Hong Kong. The defenders were outgunned and outnumbered. The mountainous terrain, thick fog, and heavy rain made defence especially difficult. All the same, the Canadians, fighting side by side with British troops, fought with exceptional bravery.

On the morning of December 19, a company of Winnipeg Rifles, led by Company Sergeant-Major John Robert Osborn, was pinned down by enemy fire for three hours on Mount Butler. The company was forced to withdraw but the men soon were surrounded by the enemy. Osborn, a veteran of the First World War, repeatedly picked up hand grenades thrown at their position and tossed them back at the Japanese. He got to one last grenade too late to grab it and fell on it instead. He was killed instantly when it exploded but saved the lives of a number of his men. The Japanese overran the position at noon.

Sergeant-Major John Robert Osborn

THE WORLD AT WAR / 55

The British governor of Hong Kong surrendered to the Japanese on Christmas Day. The British and Canadian troops who survived the fighting were sent to prisoner-of-war camps in Hong Kong and later to Japan. Conditions in the camps were terrible. Prisoners were given little to eat and no medical care. Most were forced to work as slave labour. Of those who survived until the war was over, none recovered completely from their ordeal.

They did, however, remember the courage of Sergeant-Major Osborn. When they recounted his exploits back in December 1941, Osborn was awarded the Victoria Cross posthumously.

Two hundred and ninety Canadians were killed in the defence of Hong Kong. Nearly as many died in the camps. The Japanese also lost many troops, but the Canadians were doomed from the start.

WAR DOG

At the beginning of the war, the Royal Rifles of Canada adopted as their mascot a big Newfoundland dog. They called it Gander.

Gander liked military life. He soon was made an honorary sergeant and marched on parade with the other soldiers. When the Royal Rifles went to Hong Kong in 1941, Gander went too. Gander's battalion defended the beaches at Lye Mun Gap when the Japanese landed. A fellow soldier left the dog with a group of wounded Canadians, hoping the dog would be safe there. Gander twice stopped advancing Japanese soldiers by chasing them away. In a final act of heroism, Gander gathered up a Japanese grenade just before it exploded. He was awarded the Dickin Medal posthumously. The medal recognizes "conspicuous gallantry and devotion to duty" by any animal serving with British Commonwealth forces.

Left: The Canadians who survived the Japanese prisoner-of-war camps were half-starved and psychologically scarred by the experience.

THE SHEEP DOG NAVY

As the powerful German forces vanquished Allied armies in Europe, and drove the British back across the English Channel, another campaign was being fought on the high seas.

The Allies knew that they would have to return to continental Europe one day if they were going to win the war. Only Britain could provide the base from which the invasion of Europe could be launched. But Britain didn't have enough factories to make all the guns and ammunition, tanks and warplanes, as well as all the other supplies, that would be needed for victory. Nor did it have enough troops. These resources would come from Canada and the United States. The only way to get them to Britain was by ship. The only route was across the North Atlantic. If the ships kept coming, the Allies had a chance.

The Germans knew this. And they knew that the Allies had no real defence against undersea attack. In 1939, Hitler's navy had 57 U-boats. It was fortunate for the Allies that they didn't have more. With more U-boats, the German navy might have won the war at sea before the Allies learned to fight back. As it was, the merchant marine lost an enormous number of ships. By some estimates, one out of four merchant sailors died in the war.

Canada's navy had 11 ships in 1939: none was equipped for anti-submarine warfare. In 1940, Canada's shipyards started building 64 ships specially designed for hunting U-boats. These "corvettes" became the sheep dogs that herded the convoys of merchant ships that kept Britain in the war.

Left: The minesweeper *Clayoquot* was sunk by a U-boat near Halifax on Christmas Eve, 1944. The survivors were rescued by the corvette *Fennel*.
Above: Corvettes had very little space for the crew to relax in.

CONVOY SC42

Convoys took terrible losses in the early years of the war. Canadian crews were new at their job. They were badly outclassed by the enemy.

Convoy SC42, guarded by Canadian corvettes, encountered a German U-boat wolf pack off Greenland in early September 1941. The escort commander called for reinforcements and two more corvettes, HMCS *Chambly* and *Moose Jaw*, set sail from St. John's, Newfoundland, to help out. Before they arrived, however, the U-boats attacked the convoy, sinking several merchant vessels. The escorts, unsure how to respond, spent more time picking up survivors than in looking for the enemy. More ships went down.

Five days after the first attack, *Chambly* and *Moose Jaw* approached the edge of the convoy and surprised one of the U-boats, U-501. *Chambly* dropped depth charges. The U-boat surfaced so close to *Moose Jaw* that its captain leapt onto the corvette's deck. He wanted to surrender, to save the lives of his crew, but his crew had other ideas. The U-boat started to pull away and *Moose Jaw* rammed it. The U-boat sank soon after it was struck. Eleven Germans and one Canadian went down with the sub. It was the first confirmed sinking of a U-boat by the RCN in the war.

The victory gave little comfort to the Allies. Fifteen of the 64 merchant ships in the convoy were sunk.

Opposite: The corvette *Battleford* buries its bow in the North Atlantic in November 1941.
Opposite, top: Depth charges, rolled from ramps on the rear deck of a corvette, explode in the water.

HEAVY GOING

A corvette was armed with a 4-inch gun, an anti-aircraft gun, and assorted machine guns, but its principal weapon was depth charges. These were explosive-filled drums that were either dropped from the stern or fired over the sides by "Hedgehogs" (below). Corvettes were tough, cheap, and easy to build, but they bucked like steers when the waves were heavy. They plowed into steep waves rather than riding them. Men were often swept overboard. Countless crewmen were injured when they were thrown against a bulkhead or rail. For those who sailed in corvettes, U-boats must sometimes have seemed a minor inconvenience compared with the daily bruising they experienced on their own ships.

THE GRIMMEST WINTER

U-boat wolf packs slaughtered the merchant ships like sheep. The winter of 1942–43 was the worst. That November, 119 Allied ships went down. Fewer were lost in December and January because the weather was too foul even for U-boats. Then the losses spiked again: 63 ships were sunk in February, 108 in March. Two convoys that spring lost a quarter of their number in three terrible days. Meanwhile, Canadian warships had sunk just four U-boats in all 1942. That winter, they sank none.

SO LONG

Canadians troops had been sent to Britain to fight. Instead they waited. General McNaughton insisted that his army could not be broken up: they would fight together or not at all. But the British had no use for an entire army. So, while Canadian troops waited in Britain, their allies fought against the Germans in Africa and Greece. Hitler broke his pact with Stalin in June 1941 and attacked Russia, which then entered the war on the Allied side. The United States joined in after Pearl Harbor. The Canadians still waited. When, finally, the British suggested that Canadians take part in a raid on the French coast, McNaughton agreed.

DIEPPE

The town of Dieppe, France, was heavily defended by the occupying Germans. The first plan for the raid had a number of elements. First, cruisers would bombard the town from the sea. Then the air force would bomb it from the sky. Paratroopers would be dropped behind the defenders. Finally, infantry, supported by tanks, would land on the beaches. But then the plan changed.

The Royal Navy refused to bring its big ships so close to shore-based artillery. The bombers were busy elsewhere. The paratroop operation was cancelled. British commandos were assigned to take the gun emplacements instead. That left the infantry to achieve its objectives with the support of a few destroyers and six squadrons of fighter bombers. Instead of relying on overwhelming force, the Allies now hoped to win by surprise. Two brigades from Canada's 2nd Division, together with the Calgary Tank Regiment, boarded landing craft on the night of August

Below: Tanks and armoured vehicles were stuck and abandoned on the beach at Dieppe. Inset, left: Some of the few Canadians who made it back to England after the raid.

18, 1942. Things started to go wrong almost immediately. The ships and landing craft encountered a German convoy in the early morning. There was an exchange of fire. The Germans in Dieppe heard the explosions and manned the defences. The element of surprise had been lost. The Allied forces landed at five locations along a 16-kilometre shoreline. The commandos' targets were on either side of the port. The Canadians landed at Pourville to the west, Puy to east, and Dieppe in the middle.

The commandos on the eastern side came under heavy fire. They managed to attack but not destroy the guns that commanded the beaches. The Royal Regiment of Canada, landing at Puy, was stopped by lacerating gun and mortar fire. One company of Royals lost all but a dozen of 120 men in a matter of minutes. The assault on the western side fared a little better. The commandos silenced their target, a coastal battery. Some Canadian units were landed on the wrong side of a bridge leading to Dieppe. Lieutenant-Colonel Cecil Merritt of the South Saskatchewan Regiment led his men across the bridge through a ferocious fusillade. "Come on over," he yelled to his men. "There's nothing to it." He was awarded a Victoria Cross for his daring. His unit, however, was unable to achieve its objective. It took heavy losses when it attempted to withdraw.

The main attack was a disaster. Tanks got stuck on the pebble beach or were stopped by anti-tank obstacles. A few units of infantry staggered to the seawall through the storm of bullets. One platoon of the Royal Hamilton Light Infantry fought its way into town but was forced back. Most of the first wave and the reinforcements that followed were pinned down on the beach. Withdrawal was impossible. Of the roughly 5,000 Canadians who embarked for Dieppe, more than 900 were killed, and more than 1,800 were taken prisoner.

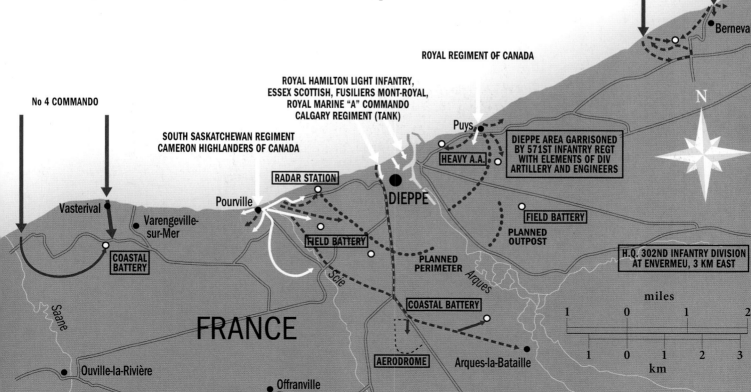

THE HOME FRONT

Tens of thousands of Canadians went overseas to fight against fascism. Things changed for the families they left behind. People at home became part of the war effort, too. The war affected everything from the food they ate and the clothes they wore to the jobs they worked at.

The war at sea meant that food items imported from other countries, such as sugar, tea, and coffee, were in short supply. Families were rationed: they were told by the government how much of each item they could buy. Gasoline, which was needed for military purposes, also was rationed. Even cloth was scarce. Government booklets gave instructions for cutting up old coats to make new clothes. The amount of fabric used to make a suit or skirt was regulated to save material. Canadians were told to "Use it up, wear it out, make it do, or do without."

DIG IN and DIG OUT the SCRAP

Save
METALS RAGS PAPER BONES RUBBER GLASS
THEY ARE VITAL WAR NEEDS
GET IN TOUCH WITH YOUR LOCAL COMMITTEE

Items that previously were considered garbage now were saved. Children collected old pots and pans. The metal could be reused by factories making tanks, guns, and ammunition. Cooks set aside bones that could be turned into glue for airplanes. Schools organized paper drives. Newspapers had fewer pages because paper was needed for the war effort.

Women had to fill many of the jobs that men used to perform because so many men were overseas. Close to a million women went to work. Almost a third of them worked in factories that made guns, ships, fighter planes, and military vehicles, not just for Canadians, but for Allied countries, too. Many factories operated on three shifts, 24 hours a day. Women could not work these hours and look after children, so some factories provided daycare.

All three branches of the armed services made room for women in support roles. More than 20,000 women joined the Canadian Women's Army Corps (CWAC); about 17,000 joined the RCAF Women's Division; and 6,000 joined the Women's Royal Canadian Naval Service (WRCNS). Together they proved that women could perform a variety of jobs that used to be for men only.

Women were contributing mightily to winning the war. However, they were not yet treated as equals by men. Women usually were paid less than men doing the same jobs. Managers and shift bosses were almost all men. The war gave women new opportunities, but there was still a long way to go.

Opposite page: Boys collect rubber to be recycled for the war effort while a couple in Toronto cultivates their victory garden. Meanwhile (right) thousands of women joined the armed services.

QUEEN OF THE HURRICANES

Elsie MacGill was the first woman in Canada to earn a university degree as an electrical engineer. As an engineer with the Canadian Car and Foundry Company, which manufactured the Hawker Hurricane fighter plane in Canada, she refined the plane's design. At the company's factory in Fort William (now Thunder Bay), Ontario, she was in charge of thousands of workers (almost half of them women) who made approximately 1,400 planes during the war. She was so famous that she was even featured in a comic book called *Queen of the Hurricanes* (right). She achieved all this even though she was partly disabled. She'd had polio when she was younger and walked with canes and leg braces the rest of her life.

A Hawker Hurricane in flight (top)
and being refuelled in England (below).

AIR DYNAMICS

Canada kept the Canadian army separate from the British. The new Royal Canadian Air Force (RCAF), however, meshed with the Royal Air Force. Canadians, either as members of the RAF or in RCAF squadrons working with the RAF, took part in all kinds of air operations from 1940 until the end of the war.

SO MUCH, SO MANY, SO FEW

No. 1 Fighter Squadron was the first unit of the RCAF to take on the German Luftwaffe. The squadron's Hawker Hurricanes tangled with German bombers over southern England on August 26, 1940. The Canadians shot down three and damaged four others. This was the height of the Battle of Britain, when from July until the end of September, Hitler attempted to vanquish Britain's air defences by shooting down its planes and bombing its airfields. Britain came close to defeat. Canadian pilots played a part in its defence. Winston Churchill famously paid tribute to all who fought in the campaign, saying, "Never in the field of human conflict was so much owed by so many to so few."

The Canadian squadron counted 31 enemy kills. It damaged or destroyed an additional 43 German aircraft. It lost three pilots and 16 planes.

At the end of September 1940, Hitler changed his strategy. He sent the Luftwaffe to bomb London. Wave after wave of German bombers dropped explosives on the city from October until May 1941. The result was death and devastation, but Londoners took pride in surviving the "Blitz."

Above: A recruiting poster.
Below: The Canadian crew of a Lancaster bomber poses in front of their aircraft in 1944. They were part of the 428 "Ghost" Squadron.

BOMBS AWAY

Beginning in 1942, Britain's air force took the war to the enemy. Masses of bombers attacked industrial and military targets in Germany. Later in the war, they also bombed cities. More than half a million people were killed in these raids, most of them civilians. No one doubted that the bombing was necessary. Canadians were a part of it and they lost many planes and men. Daylight raids were especially dangerous. Night raids were safer but it was harder to identify targets. Canadians continued to volunteer to serve in the RCAF throughout the war.

In 1943, several Canadian bomber squadrons were brought together to form No. 6 Group, RCAF, based in the north of England. The group had problems at first. They were among the last groups to get new planes. They were flying two-engine Wellingtons when most other groups were flying newer four-engine Halifax and Lancaster aircraft. Their training and morale lagged behind the others. Air Vice-Marshal "Black Mike" McEwan took over in 1944. He pressed for better training and equipment. By the end of the year, the Canadian group was the most accurate in the RAF. And it took the fewest casualties.

Left: An Allied bomber over Germany.
Opposite page: Miller Brittain's painting, *Night Target, Germany*, shows the confusing and strangely beautiful spectacle of Allied bombers flying through enemy searchlights and anti-aircraft fire.

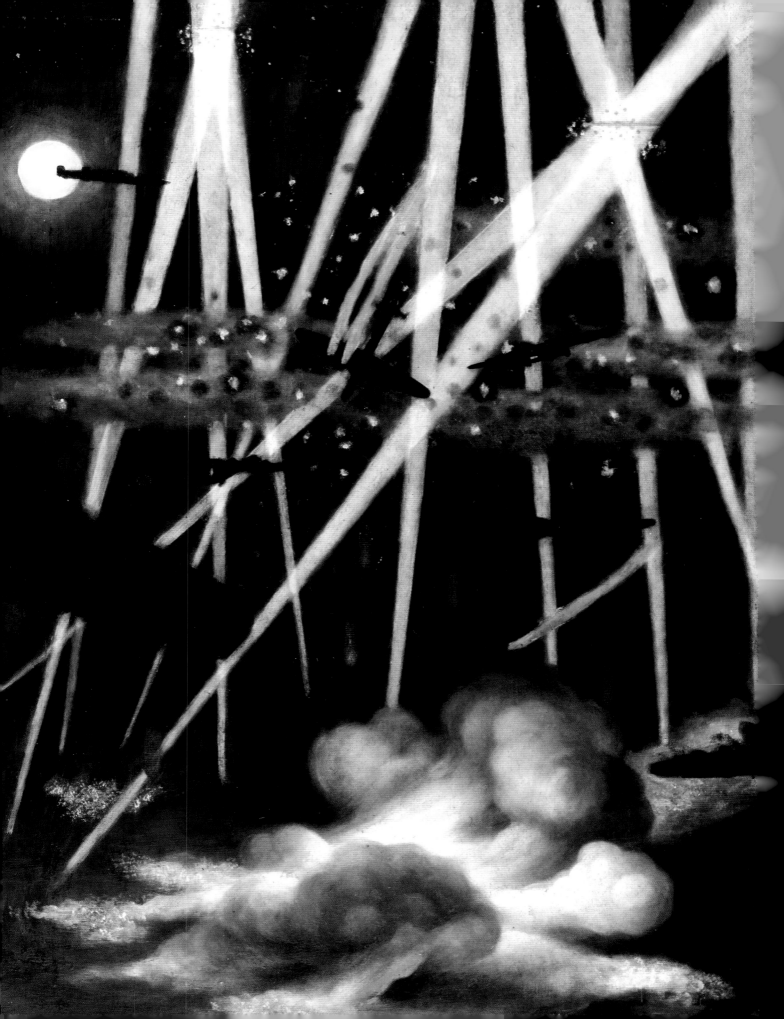

INFANTRY ORGANIZATION

Armies are complex organizations that change with evolving conditions and technology. The First Canadian Army, commanded by a full general, consisted of two corps. An army corps was commanded by a lieutenant-general and consisted of from two to five divisions. A division was commanded by a major-general and consisted usually of three brigades. A brigade was commanded by a brigadier or colonel and consisted of three or more battalions. A battalion was commanded by a lieutenant-colonel and consisted of four or more companies. A company was commanded by a major or captain and consisted of from 100 to 200 soldiers formed into platoons. A platoon was led by a lieutenant and consisted of a maximum of about 30 or 40 men, typically divided into eight-man sections.

Above: Canadian troops enter Dieppe in September 1944.
Opposite page: Soldiers of the Hasty Ps in Sicily, July 1943.

EUROPE'S SOFT UNDERBELLY

The year 1942 marked a turning point for the Allies. There had been terrible setbacks in North Africa and the Far East. The Atlantic war was going very badly. The Luftwaffe was still strong. But then the British won an important tank battle at El Alamein, Egypt. Next, British and American forces landed in Tunisia, Algeria, and Morocco, and the stage was set for victory in North Africa. Meanwhile, Hitler's advance into Soviet Russia was stopped at Stalingrad as bitter cold and winter snow overwhelmed his armies.

Soviet Premier Joseph Stalin wanted the Allies to invade Europe. This would force Hitler to fight the war on two fronts. Neither Churchill nor American president Franklin Roosevelt was ready for an all-out invasion. Churchill proposed instead that Allied forces strike at "the soft underbelly of the Axis," meaning the occupied European countries on the Mediterranean Sea. Canada was asked to contribute some of its army for an attack on Sicily, an Italian island off the southwestern tip of the country. General McNaughton opposed the plan. He wanted to save the army for the invasion of northern Europe. Mackenzie King was worried that the war would end without Canada's army playing a major part and overruled him.

American troops landed on the western coast of the island of Sicily on July 10, 1943. Britain's 8th Army, including the 1st Canadian Infantry Division and the 1st Armoured Brigade, landed on the eastern side. They were opposed by the Italian 6th Army, plus two German divisions supported by tanks. The battle for the island lasted five weeks.

THE TAKING OF ASSORO

The Hastings and Prince Edward Regiment (or "Hasty Ps") landed near Cape Passero, on Sicily, on July 10. They encountered almost no resistance on the beach and were ordered to proceed inland. Conditions were difficult: the men faced swarms of flies, oppressive heat, and steep mountain terrain. They soon faced tough resistance as well.

The town of Assoro, with its narrow streets and old stone buildings, occupied one end of a high ridge. Canadian scouts led by the unit's commanding officer, Lieutenant-Colonel Bruce Sutcliffe, came under German fire on July 20. Sutcliffe was killed. His second-in-command, Major John "Long John" Buchan, son of Canada's late governor general, took over.

That night, Buchan led his troops up a steep mountain path in darkness and nearly total silence. After a nerve-wracking, 40-minute climb, the Hasty Ps found themselves beside the ruins of a great Norman castle on the mountaintop. They quickly overpowered a German observation post. From this position, they directed artillery fire on the Germans in the town below. With support from the Royal Canadian Regiment and the 48th Highlanders, the Hasty Ps took Assoro by noon on July 22.

The battle of Assoro broke the German line, though the Germans kept on fighting. They set ambushes, held defensive positions as long as possible, and then pulled back. The Canadians took one town after another, often suffering heavy casualties. Sicily was in Allied hands by August 17. The battle for the Italian mainland lay ahead.

THE ITALIAN BOOT

Mussolini was overthrown by his own country-men before Sicily fell. Soon after, in September 1943, the Italian government surrendered. The Germans, however, were determined to slow down the Allied advance. Under Field Marshal Albert Kesselring, the German army used Italy's natural mountain fortresses and deep river valleys to deadly effect.

The Apennine mountains run the length of the Italian mainland. American forces worked their way up the western slopes. British and Canadian forces attacked the eastern side. It was a brutal campaign. A summer of stifling heat and choking dust was followed by a cold and miserable winter. Hardly a single town was taken without losses. Some were the scene of unbridled slaughter.

ORTONA

In November 1943, the 1st Division was assigned to take the town of Ortona at the eastern end of the Gustav Line. To get there, the Canadians first had to cross the Moro River, then negotiate a deep valley, and finally climb onto the main road leading into the town. At every stage, they came under devastating fire from well-positioned machine-gun nests, as well as mortars and tanks. The river crossing alone was a tough test. Units of the Hasty Ps crossed once, were pushed back, and crossed again over two terrifying days and nights in early December. Finally, engineers constructed a temporary bridge and the Canadians were able to bring across light tanks and troop carriers. They fought for another week before attacking the town itself.

Right: Canadian forces advance on the Hitler Line, May 1944.
Inset: A Canadian sniper with the 48th Highlanders takes aim at a German position.

Stone-sided buildings stood shoulder to shoulder on Ortona's narrow streets. The Germans knocked some down to give a clear field of fire for machine guns. They buried tanks in the rubble, creating an impenetrable apron of stone around the turrets and their deadly cannons. Streets were blocked to form traps.

The Loyal Edmonton Regiment and Seaforth Highlanders engaged the enemy at the edge of town on December 10. For two weeks, they and other units from the Canadian 1st Division fought a bloody non-stop battle. The streets were so dangerous that the Canadians took to "mouse-holing." They moved from one house to the next by blowing holes in the side walls. They fought through Christmas Day. To keep up morale, support units served Christmas dinner in church courtyards. Men dropped out of the battle for an hour, enjoyed their holiday meal, and then went back to the shooting. Sometimes they found themselves face-to-face with their enemy and the fighting was hand-to-hand. Finally, a few days after Christmas, the Germans withdrew. Ortona belonged to the Canadians.

GETTING TO GUSTAV

The Canadians had landed in Italy in early September 1943. They encountered light resistance at Potenza. In mid-October, they took another town, Campobasso, after a tougher fight. These engagements followed a familiar pattern: the Germans held their positions as

Top left: The battle for Ortona in December 1943 was one of the toughest fought by the Canadians in Italy.
Bottom left: Charles Comfort's painting, *Via Dolorosa, Ortona*, shows the ruins that remained when the fighting ended.

long as possible. And then, when the Allies applied enough pressure, they disappeared into the night.

Things changed when the Allies approached the Gustav Line. This was a string of defences that Kesselring had constructed across Italy, about 120 kilometres south of Rome. Here the Germans made a stand.

CANADA'S BREAKTHROUGH

On January 22, 1944, the Americans landed at Anzio, on Italy's western coast. They were trying to get around another German defensive barrier, the Hitler Line. The assault was almost a disaster: German forces closed in on the beachhead and trapped the Americans. The British and Canadians mounted an assault in the Liri Valley in May to take pressure off the Anzio beachhead.

The Canadians attacked the Germans at a point where the Melfa River met the Liri. Canadian General E.L.M. Burns planned to engage the enemy along a 2,000-metre front, with heavy artillery, tanks, and infantry. It was no triumph. At one point, the Lord Strathcona's Horse (now a tank regiment) fought a desperate, isolated battle with panzers until it was relieved by British forces. The campaign was successful in the end and the Hitler Line was broken. American and Free French (French soldiers in exile while France was occupied) forces liberated Rome on June 4.

Kesselring again retreated northwards with the Allies in dogged pursuit. He built yet another series of fortifications from Pisa to Rimini. With more than 2,000 machine-gun nests, hundreds of anti-tank

A RAY OF SUNSHINE

General McNaughton had a prickly personality. The British thought he was incompetent. In early 1944, he was replaced by H.D.G. "Harry" Crerar as the General Officer Commanding the Canadian army. Crerar had commanded the 1st Canadian Corps. Now General E.L.M. Burns (above, in Italy, March 1944) took his place. Burns was an intelligent but dour soldier. His men jokingly referred to him as "Smilin' Sunray."

The Canadians were still part of the British 8th Army. This was commanded by General Montgomery until the spring when his place was taken by General Sir Oliver Leese. Leese, like many British generals, looked down on "colonial" troops. When things did not go well, he was quick to blame the colonials, although often the failings were his own.

"FOUR YEARS AGO WHEN I JOINED UP I KNEW NOTHING AT ALL ABOUT COOKIN'!"

"NICE LITTLE KIDS, EH HERBIE!"

HERBIE

"Herbie" was created by graphic artist Bing Coughlin. He appeared for the first time in the armed forces magazine *Maple Leaf* in spring 1944. Both Coughlin and his character Herbie served with Canadian forces in Italy and western Europe. Herbie was an innocent and a survivor, a long-suffering foot-slogger with no respect for authority. In 1944, Canadian soldiers voted Herbie Man of the Year.

guns, and scores of tank turrets half-buried in concrete, the Gothic Line was a final, formidable obstacle.

At the end of August, the Allies were ready to crack it. The Canadians were assigned to clear the Germans from the region between the Metaura and Foglia Rivers. They made rapid progress. The 5th Armoured Division, commanded by Major-General B.M. Hoffmeister, achieved its objective. Hoffmeister, scouting ahead, noticed that there were few German forces in front of him. On his own initiative, he drove his tanks through open territory and turned behind the German defences. It was a brilliant and daring move. It showed how much the Canadians had learned since the battle at Melfa. But the Germans regrouped and the battle for Italy continued on into the fall.

EXIT STRATEGY

Although the fighting in Italy wasn't finished, the Canadians were pulled out in December 1944. More than 90,000 had served there. Nearly 6,000 were killed, some 20,000 wounded, and 1,000 taken prisoner.

On the Eastern Front, Soviet Russia had inflicted a series of crushing defeats on Hitler's armies, notably in an epic tank battle at Kursk. By the spring of 1944, it was clear that Soviet armies would move on Germany's borders before the year was out. The Western Allies prepared to open a new front in northern Europe.

CHEZ ALPHONSE

Lucien Dumais was a tough French Canadian who volunteered for the army in 1939. He fought with the Fusiliers Mont-Royal and was captured by the Germans at Dieppe. He escaped from prison camp and returned to England where he signed up with the British secret service. They sent him back to France to rescue Allied airmen whose planes had been shot down.

Dumais had a partner, Raymond LaBrosse, another French Canadian. Together they set up the Shelburne Line. This was a secret network of French resistance fighters and their supporters, who provided safe houses, food, clothing, and other assistance to the Allied airmen and their guides. The end of the line was a house—the house of Alphonse—on the coast of Brittany in northern France. From here, the airmen were picked up in the night by British gunboats and taken back to England to rejoin the war.

The Shelburne Line rescued more than 300 Allied airmen. It was a remarkable—and dangerous—achievement. Both Dumais and LaBrosse returned safely to Canada after the war.

TOMMY PRINCE AND THE DEVIL'S BRIGADE

Tommy Prince (above, left) was a descendant of Chief William Prince, who had led the Manitoba band of Salteaux volunteers on the Nile expedition in 1884. Like his ancestor, Tommy Prince had a brave and adventurous spirit.

He signed up in 1940. Two years later, craving more action, he volunteered for special service. He became part of an elite unit of about 1,600 men who trained for missions behind enemy lines. Known as the Devil's Brigade, its members learned to parachute, ski, and make amphibious landings. One of their first assignments was to land at Anzio with the Americans.

Prince was decorated for an exploit in February 1944 near Littoria, Italy. He was alone in an abandoned farmhouse observing a German position. He was telling the artillery officers behind him where to direct their fire. When a shell cut the telephone wire that connected them, Prince dressed himself as an Italian farmer. With the enemy watching, he found the place where the wire was broken, fixed it, and returned to his observation post. Because of his messages, four German positions were destroyed.

GIVE US THE SHIPS
WE'LL *finish* THE SUBS!

THE TIDE TURNS

The winter of 1942–43 had been a desperate time for convoys crossing the Atlantic. At the beginning of March 1943, senior naval officers from Britain, the United States, and Canada met in Washington. They divided the ocean into three sectors. The Americans took responsibility for the South Atlantic, the British for the mid-Atlantic, and the Canadians for the northwest. Rear Admiral Leonard W. Murray became the only Canadian to command a theatre of operations in the war.

A number of other changes were made that spring. In the past, naval escorts stayed with their convoys even when they were attacked. Now, groups of warships hunted U-boats as their only job.

Their equipment improved. ASDIC, a system to detect submarines by sending sound waves underwater, was refined. More sailors were trained to use it. New ships were equipped with the Hedgehog, which fired a pattern of bombs that, unlike depth charges, exploded only when they made contact with the target. The support groups became adept at working together, one attacking the sub while others kept in contact with it.

The Canadian navy got bigger. Six River Class destroyers were added and then the first of nearly 70 River Class frigates. To these were added the faster and more powerful Tribal Class destroyers. By the end of the war, Canada possessed the world's fourth-largest navy.

Experience and equipment made the navy more efficient. German Admiral Doenitz sent 23 U-boats against a convoy in November 1943. Just one merchant ship went down while three U-boats were sunk. Two Canadian corvettes, *Snowberry* and *Calgary,* helped sink them. U-boats were still a threat but they were finally on the run.

215

HAIDA AND *ATHABASKAN*

In April 1944, the Canadian destroyers *Haida* (opposite page) and *Athabaskan* were patrolling the English Channel. They chased three German destroyers through a minefield and sank one of the enemy ships. Three days later, *Athabaskan* was torpedoed and badly damaged. *Haida* laid a smokescreen to cover the stricken ship. She turned her guns on one of the two German attackers and drove the other onto the rocky coast of France. *Haida* then returned to the site where *Athabaskan* had been hit. It was too late: the ship had gone down. For much of the night, *Haida*'s captain, Harry G. DeWolf, did what he could to rescue survivors. He found 44 men. Another 83 were picked up and kept as prisoners by the Germans. *Athabaskan*'s captain and 128 members of the crew were lost.

Tribal Class Destroyer

River Class Frigate

Flower Class Corvette

THE RCAF AT SEA

Airplanes made a vital contribution to defeating the U-boats. RCAF squadrons based in Newfoundland acquired long-range Liberator bombers. RCAF units serving with Coastal Command in Britain were similarly equipped. The planes could patrol vast areas of ocean. When they sighted a U-boat, they strafed or bombed it. By the end of the war, the RCAF had accounted for 17 U-boat kills.

SAILING TO WAR

Although Canada's navy possessed other types of vessels (including minesweepers and patrol vessels) the ships that played the most significant combat role in the Second World War were its destroyers, frigates, and corvettes. Of these, the Tribal Class destroyers were the largest, fastest, and most heavily armed. They were about 115 metres from bow to stern, carried a crew of 259, and were fitted with three 4.7-inch guns, as well as torpedoes and anti-aircraft and machine guns. Frigates were designed for escort and anti-submarine duty rather than for fighting other ships. They were about 91 metres in length, carried a crew of 141, a single 4-inch gun, depth charges, and anti-aircraft and machine guns. Corvettes were just about 60 metres long and carried a crew of 90.

D-DAY: THE INVASION OF NORMANDY

There had never been anything like the armada that left the south of England on the night of June 5, 1944. Five thousand ships took on board 107,000 soldiers and 7,000 vehicles. Before they reached the other side of the English Channel, thousands of planes bombed roads and railways in France and Belgium. At the same time, thousands of paratroops dropped behind enemy lines. And then, as dawn lightened the gloom, the pounding began. The big guns on scores of battleships and cruisers took aim at the enemy's pillboxes and gun emplacements. Operation Overlord was under way.

Four years earlier, the Germans had driven the British into the sea. Now, from the sea, the British and their allies were returning.

"Move fast! Don't stop for anything. Go! Go! Go!" yelled Charles Martin of the Queen's Own Rifles. His platoon scrambled down the ramp of the landing craft onto the beach at Courseulles-sur-Mer. They came under fire immediately. The Germans were ready for them.

The Canadians were in charge of Juno Beach, one of five landing zones along a 100-kilometre stretch of France's Normandy coast. British divisions landed on either side of them. The Americans took two beaches to the west, near Cherbourg. For all who took part, it was both a terrible and awe-inspiring experience. Four years of planning, training, fighting, and dying had led to this moment. For their friends and families at home, it was the beginning of the end.

For the men on the beach, the war was far from over. Almost an entire company of the Regina Rifles was lost when its landing craft ran into a minefield. The Fort Garry Horse's Sherman tanks met deadly fire on the beach. The Queen's Own Rifles took the most brutal losses. A well-concealed German 88-mm anti-tank gun eliminated two-thirds of a platoon as they ran across the pebble beach.

Charles Martin, the man who had urged his platoon onto the beaches earlier in the day, survived the landing. His unit made it farther inland than any other from his company. As night fell, however, he started crying: more than half his men had been either wounded or killed. There was worse to come.

CHANNEL CROSSINGS

The Canadian Navy played its part in D-Day. Destroyers, including *Haida* and her sister ships, *Algonquin* and *Sioux,* cleared the Channel of enemy traffic. Canadian minesweepers opened the way for landing craft. Canadian troop ships ferried men and supplies to and from England. Five flotillas of RCN landing craft took troops, tanks, trucks, and artillery to the French shore. Altogether the Canadian Navy provided 109 vessels and 10,000 sailors to the D-Day operation.

Left: Reinforcements wade ashore after the first attackers secured a section of Juno Beach.

THE CANADIAN "KANGAROOS"

Lieutenant-General Guy Simonds, the most imaginative of Canadian commanding officers, wanted his infantry to keep up with the tanks when they went into battle. He had the cannons removed from the Priest self-propelled guns. He added steel armour for protection—and *voilà!* He invented the first armoured personnel carriers (APCs). The Canadians called them "kangaroos" because they made it possible for infantry to jump forward quickly. As APCs, they soon became part of every army's armoured fleet.

CAEN

D-Day was a success: the Allies took and held their beaches. The long march through northern Europe lay ahead. The battles that followed for control of northern France were among the bloodiest in the history of modern warfare. By the time Dieppe was liberated in September 1944, more than 5,000 Canadians had been killed.

Caen, an important French rail terminus and administrative centre, was just inland from the British and Canadian beaches. The Allies had meant to seize it a few days after D-Day. It took a lot longer.

The North Nova Scotia Highlanders and the 27th Canadian Armoured Regiment ran into the 12th SS Panzer Division the day after the landings. Many of the German troops were members of the Hitler Youth. Their officers, however, were veterans: some of them had fought the Russians on the Eastern Front. Both officers and youths resisted the Canadians with bitter determination.

Over five days, from June 7 to 11, Canadians were engaged in a series of intense battles. Sometimes they gained and sometimes they lost ground to the enemy. The last battle in the series, at Le Mesnil-Patry, was a disaster. Nineteen Sherman tanks of the 1st Hussars were incinerated after being hit by panzers and 88s. Only two Canadian tanks escaped. The weary Canadians were taken out of the line to rest and regroup.

At the beginning of July, they were in action again. The 3rd Infantry Division launched an attack on the town of Carpiquet and its airport south of Caen. The Germans were hit by a heavy artillery barrage before the battle—one observer described it as a "true inferno." The Germans gave up the town

but held the airport for several more days. British and Canadian troops entered Caen on July 8. They still had to deal with German snipers, mines, and booby traps. The city itself was badly damaged.

The Germans gave up nothing easily. Early in the campaign, at Buron, the Highland Light Infantry of Canada lost more than 250 men in ferocious fighting. Buron, France, like Caen, was devastated.

STALEMATE

The Germans found it easy to defend the villages of Normandy, with their stone buildings and low stone walls, and the farmers' fields around them. Hitler ordered his generals to hold on at any cost.

The Allies gained ground a bit at time. The 2nd Canadian Corps took Vaucelles and Colombelles in mid-July. Neither victory came cheaply. On July 19, elements of the Black Watch Regiment crossed the Orne River on their way to Verrières Ridge. They made good progress—until the rain began. Then Allied fighter planes were grounded and Canadian artillery could no longer find their targets. The Black Watch was pushed back. Two companies of the Fusiliers Mont-Royal went in and were almost completely destroyed. The Black Watch counterattacked but only managed to hold fast. The Canadians regrouped and attacked the ridge again. This time, the South Saskatchewan and Essex Scottish regiments were battered by the German defenders. The Black Watch, supported by two armoured regiments, managed to regain the ground that was lost. The town of Verrières—but not the ridge—was taken on July 25.

Caen was badly damaged by the fighting, as shown in Will Ogilvie's painting, *Convoy in Caen*, top, and in the photograph of troops entering the city at bottom.

CLOSING THE GAP

In August 1944, there was a chance to end the stalemate in Normandy. The Americans broke out of their beachhead in the west. They were moving fast on a course behind the German divisions on the coast. If the British and Canadians moved just as swiftly from Caen south to Falaise, they could trap the Germans and bring an end to the Normandy campaign.

Lieutenant-General Guy Simonds planned a two-phase operation, called Totalize, that began with a heavy barrage on the night of August 7. In the morning, the infantry rode behind the tanks on armoured personnel carriers. The attackers made a hole in the German line. Then they stopped to regroup, and the Germans launched a counterattack. The second phase was less successful. "Worthington Force"—the 28th Armoured Regiment with two companies of infantry—got lost. It was surrounded and beaten up: 240 Canadians were killed; 47 of their tanks were destroyed.

Canadian troops enter Falaise, August 1944.

A week later, Simonds pressed on toward Falaise in Operation Tractable. The village was taken on August 16. The gap between Simonds's army and the Americans was closed five days later. It was a messy victory: Allied planes bombed and strafed German units on the ground. Thousands of Germans were either killed or taken prisoner. But thousands more slipped away before the trap snapped shut.

SAINT-LAMBERT

In the last days of the battle for Normandy, the Canadians fought an epic battle at Saint-Lambert-sur-Dives. Units from the South Alberta Regiment and the Argyll and Sutherland Highlanders stood alone to stem the flow of fleeing Germans on the last road out of Falaise. It was a desperate business. The officer commanding the South Albertas squadron, Major D.V. Currie, lost all his officers. Yet he single-handedly destroyed a Tiger tank while exhorting his men to keep on fighting. In the end, his small band captured some 2,000 Germans.

THE SCHELDT

On September 3, 1944, Canadians marched proudly—and sadly—into Dieppe, scene of the terrible battle two years before. In the weeks that followed, they took three more French cities along the coast: Boulogne, Calais, and Le Havre.

Four months after the invasion, supplies still were being shipped from Britain to France by way of temporary docks on the Normandy beaches. From there, they were moved hundreds of kilometres by truck to the advancing armies. The Allies needed a port closer to the action. They acquired one when the British seized Antwerp in Belgium. But the British neglected to clear the part of the Scheldt River that led to the city from the sea. The Germans built fortifications, flooded fields, and prepared to hold out against attackers. The Canadians were given the job of forcing them out.

Canadian troops cross the Scheldt River, September 1944.

The battle for the Scheldt estuary was an exhausting and costly struggle. As in Normandy, progress was slow. General Simonds needed more men and tanks than he had been given. Finally, in mid-October, the British gave him two additional divisions. They made a huge difference. At the end of November, the first Allied merchant ship—a Canadian freighter—sailed into Antwerp's harbour.

THE LAST WINTER

By the winter of 1944–45, there was almost no chance that the remaining Axis powers—Germany and Japan—could win the war. The Gothic Line in Italy was shattered. Soviet armies were marching on the Third Reich from the east. In the west, Hitler launched a last desperate counterattack. The Battle of the Bulge was fought mainly against American troops in bitter winter conditions. The Germans were beaten back. Meanwhile, in the Pacific, the United States Marines were about to land on the island of Iwo Jima, which could be used as a base for attacking Japan.

That winter, the Canadians held a position on the Dutch-German border. They skirmished with the enemy but participated in no major operations until the early spring.

CLEARING THE RHINELAND

In February 1945, Canadians were assigned the task of punching a path roughly from Nijmegen, Netherlands, to Wesel, Germany. Their path ran between the Maas and Rhine rivers and through the Reichswald Forest, the Siegfried Line, and the Hochwald Forest. The Germans were fighting in their homeland for the first time. They resisted the Allied advance with everything they had.

Canadians showed courage and resourcefulness throughout the operation. A platoon of the Queen's Own Rifles, with two tanks, approached three farmhouses near the village of Mooshof, Germany, on February 26, 1945. Enemy fire knocked out one tank and killed or wounded all but five members of the platoon. Sergeant Aubrey Cosens took command. He ran across open ground to the remaining tank, ordered it to ram one of the farm buildings, and followed it in. He either killed or took prisoner the enemy soldiers hiding inside. He then entered the remaining two buildings in the same manner. He was killed by a sniper after the skirmish.

Some Canadian forces crossed the Rhine in pursuit of the Germans. In early March, the Highland Light Infantry won a fierce battle at Speldrop, Germany. By the end of the month, however, the Canadians were back in Holland.

THE CAMPS

George Blackburn was an officer with the 4th Field Regiment, Royal Canadian Artillery, when his unit liberated the Westerbork concentration camp near Assen, Holland. More than 100,000 Jews, including the 15-year-old diarist Anne Frank, had passed through this camp on their way to Poland and Germany where they were systematically killed. Blackburn later recalled the look of "pure, raw joy" in the eyes of the prisoners, starving and ill, who surrounded his vehicles. He and his men could only pass out their chocolate bars, loaves of bread, and cans of food before pressing on in pursuit of the retreating enemy.

Canadian troops had heard rumours about the concentration camps. Few had believed them. The awful discovery of this and other camps came as a profound shock.

Left: In the battle on the Dutch-German border, a Canadian soldier takes aim against the enemy.
Inset: Gunners prepare to fire a twenty-five pounder.

THE LIBERATION OF HOLLAND

In the last months of the war, the 1st Canadian Infantry and 5th Armoured Division were moved from Italy to northern Europe. Finally, the two Canadian corps were united in a single army. Their task was to drive the remaining Germans out of Holland. The 1st Canadian Corps set out to clear the western part of the country starting at Arnhem, where British forces had already seen fierce combat. The Germans fought for every house. By the time the Canadians won the city, few buildings had escaped damage. The Canadians paused before pushing on. Some 120,000 German troops awaited them, but everyone knew the war would end soon. Meanwhile, Dutch civilians were starving. The Allies negotiated a truce with the Germans. The fighting stopped, and the Germans allowed the Allies to deliver food to the Dutch people.

The task of the 2nd Canadian Corps was to drive through northern Holland to Germany and the Weser River. Sometimes the going was easy. At other times, the Canadians met stiff resistance. Some of the fiercest battles were fought against Dutch Nazis. They knew they faced harsh punishment from their compatriots after the war was over. The war finally ended on May 7, 1945, when German commanders surrendered to the Allies at Rheims in Northern France. The 2nd Corps, which had been poised to move on the German town of Wilhelmshaven, stood down.

Residents of Leeuwarden, Holland, welcome the Canadian troops.

WAR BRIDES

Rosalind Elder was dismayed when she first set eyes on Halifax in April 1946. She said the houses looked like "apple crates turned upside down. The pier looked like a cattle shed." The weather, too, was dismal, cold, and bleak. Worse was to come. Her destination was St. John's, Newfoundland, which seemed still trapped in winter. Elder was travelling from her home and family in England to join her husband in Newfoundland. Everything was different. Adjusting to the change was a challenge. War brides like Elder needed almost as much courage to survive in peace as their husbands did in war.

Hundreds of thousands of Canadian troops had been based in Britain before the invasions of Italy and France. Many met British girls and fell in love. At the end of the war, some 48,000 women—most of them British—made the journey to Canada. Elder learned to cook Newfoundland specialties such as cods' tongues and to make her own bread. Other women adjusted to life in small-town Ontario or to the isolation of the prairies. All brought something of the Old Country to add to Canada's cultural mix.

MOWAT'S MUSEUM

When the war came to an end, author Farley Mowat, then an officer with the Hasty Ps, used his time in Holland and Germany to collect as many pieces of German military equipment as he could. His collection included a V-2 rocket as well as tanks and artillery. German engineers were highly sophisticated. Many of their designs, for everything from warplanes to handguns, were superior to those used by the Allies. Their rocket technology, especially, was the best in the world. To Mowat, it made sense to keep the specimens he found so that Canadian scientists could take them apart and learn their secrets. His superior officers were not interested in his project, however. His marvellous collection was shipped back to Canada . . . and mostly junked. A few pieces ended up in the Canadian War Museum.

TOTAL VICTORY

Germany had gone through a ruinous time after the end of the Great War. Fascism had emerged from the tumult and fascism had led to war. The Allies were determined that this would never happen again.

Four armies carved up what was left of Germany in 1945. The Soviet Union seized the eastern part of the country. The Americans, British, and French took the rest. The Soviet Union installed a communist government in their sector. The Western Allies set up a democratic government in theirs. In all sectors, the Allies established an army of occupation. Germany was disarmed.

DEMOBILIZATION, DOWNSIZING

Nearly half a million Canadians returned from Europe in 1945. Some had been away for six years. All were anxious to start new lives in a world at peace.

The armed forces, however, took pride in their wartime status. The navy's top officers wanted to maintain a big-ship fleet similar to the British and Americans. The army planned on keeping a regular force of more than 50,000 soldiers and as many again in training or in reserve. The RCAF envisioned a permanent force of some 30,000. The government, however, agreed with the returning veterans: they looked forward to peace. The wish list of all three services was chopped in half.

Canada contributed 25,000 troops and 11 RCAF squadrons to the British occupation forces in Germany in 1945. In 1946, despite British objections, they all came home.

THE NUREMBERG TRIALS

Hitler committed suicide at the end of April 1945. Some of his henchmen, however, either surrendered or were captured. Reichsmarschall Hermann Goering and the minister of industrial production, Albert Speer, were among the Germans who were tried before an Allied military tribunal at Nuremberg, Germany. They were charged with various crimes including conspiracy to wage aggressive war, war crimes, and crimes against humanity.

The trials were meant to show that the Nazis were criminals. The Nuremberg Trials introduced the idea that states could commit crimes against humanity. This idea gained significance in the years that followed.

Above: Nazis on trial at Nuremberg. Hermann Goering is in the front row, far left.
Left: Canadians gather on Parliament Hill and (inset) on Sparks Street in Ottawa to celebrate the end of the war, May 1945.

THE CURTAIN FALLS

The world in 1945 was very different from the world of 1939. For Canadians, and soon for most of Western Europe, it was a more prosperous place. Just as importantly, the balance of power had shifted. Britain no longer presided over a far-flung empire: its former colonies were going their own way. In Britain's place, America emerged as the wealthiest and most powerful western nation. At the same time, the Soviet Union became the superpower of the East. In time, the Soviets would be challenged by another eastern state, China. By 1949, communist revolutionaries in China would drive American-backed Nationalists onto the island of Taiwan.

Everyone could see that Western Europe was no longer the centre of the world's military, financial, and trading might. Europe itself was up for grabs. The Soviet Union treated the countries its armies had invaded when they were pursuing the Germans as colonies. The Baltic states, plus Poland, Hungary, Bulgaria, Albania, Yugoslavia, and Romania—along with East Germany—all fell within the new Soviet empire. This communist Soviet Union was hostile to the democratic West. Each side feared the other. In a speech in 1946, Winston Churchill spoke of the "Iron Curtain" that divided Europe. An American diplomat called for a strategy to "contain" Soviet aggression. Two years later, the Soviet Union took over Czechoslovakia. It then attempted to drive the Western powers out of Germany's divided capital, Berlin.

The city was entirely inside the Soviet-controlled half of Germany. The Soviets imposed a blockade to stop Westerners from gaining access. The West, led by the United States, mounted a rescue operation to keep their part of the city open. They flew planes with food and supplies in and out of Berlin's airport. The Soviets finally lifted the blockade in 1949, but the Cold War had begun.

THE MUSHROOM CLOUD

On August 6, 1945, an American B-29 bomber dropped an atomic bomb on the Japanese city of Hiroshima. Three days later, a similar bomb was dropped on Nagasaki. Tens of thousands of people died instantly. The Japanese quickly surrendered. These bombs were more powerful by far than any weapon the world had known.

At first, only the United States knew how to make the bomb. Then Soviet scientists discovered the secret. People everywhere were frightened that the two superpowers would use the bomb against each other. The atomic bomb cast a dark shadow over the world in the Cold War.

GOUZENKO

Igor Gouzenko was a cipher clerk in the Soviet embassy in Ottawa. He was scheduled to go home to Russia. He didn't want to go. He liked what he saw of Canada, its freedom and prosperity. He decided to defect.

On the morning of September 5, 1945, he stuffed a bunch of documents under his shirt and into his pockets. The documents showed that a few Canadians were passing secrets to the Soviet Union. Gouzenko smuggled the documents out of the embassy. For the next two days, he tried hard to get someone to pay attention to him.

On the first day, he showed the papers to journalists, the RCMP, and government officials. No one was interested. On the second day, he tried , and failed, to gain an interview with the minister of justice. At last, exhausted and scared, he returned to his apartment building. He realized that officials at the embassy now knew he had run away. He was certain they would send agents to have him kidnapped or killed. He persuaded neighbours to let him stay in their apartment for the night. It was a wise move. Soviet agents broke into his apartment at midnight. And then, at last, the police took him seriously and offered him protection.

Gouzenko's revelations shook not only Ottawa, but also London and Washington. The Canadian spy ring had connections in both Britain and the United States. Tensions already existed between East and West: after Gouzenko, the tensions were worse.

Opposite page: Berliners watch a military transport plane bringing relief supplies into the city in 1948.

THE UN VOTES FOR WAR

The Allies created the United Nations after the end of the war. They hoped it would bring about world peace. A small group of countries made up the Security Council within the United Nations to deal with emergencies. Both the United States and the Soviet Union (but not communist China) were members of the Security Council.

On June 25, 1950, communist North Korean troops crossed the border from North into South Korea. The United States introduced a resolution to the Security Council condemning the aggression. The resolution passed because the Soviet Union, which would have supported North Korea, did not attend the meeting. The Security Council authorized the United States to take the lead in opposing the attack.

THE CHINESE INTERVENE

Korean, American, and British troops had been surprised by the North Korean attack. By mid-July, they had retreated all the way south to the port of Pusan. Then, on September 15, Americans landed troops behind North Korean lines at Inchon. It was the turn of the North Koreans to retreat. They withdrew all the way north to the Yalu River, which forms part of the border with China. The American commander, General Douglas MacArthur, announced that the war was all but over. He was wrong.

China, North Korea's ally, gathered its forces on the other side of the Yalu. On November 26, the Chinese counterattacked. The Americans and their allies again were surprised by the strength and fierceness of the enemy. Many of the Chinese troops

Troops of the Princess Pats on patrol in Korea, March 1951.

PLANES OVER KOREA

Eighteen Canadian pilots served in the United States Air Force in Korea. They flew Sabre jet fighters and shot down nine Russian-built MiGs. They are credited with two "probable" enemy kills and with having damaged ten more.

Above: Canadian airmen at a base in Korea, March 1951.
Right: A machine-gun crew from the Royal Canadian Regiment.

had been fighting for years, against the Japanese and against Chinese Nationalists in the civil war: they were battle-hardened soldiers. The UN forces retreated, made a stand, and retreated again. The Chinese took South Korea's capital city, Seoul, before their advance came to a halt in January 1951.

ROUGH DIAMONDS AND HARD CASES

Canada sent three destroyers to Korea as soon as the war began. Then the government sent a squadron of transport planes. Finally, it decided to raise an expeditionary force (that is, one that could be sent overseas). The Canadian Army Special Force was made up of volunteers. Three battalions were formed in each

of the regular force infantry units: the Princess Pats, the RCR, and the Royal 22nd (the Van Doos). These battalions became the first Canadian brigade.

Not all the volunteers made good soldiers. Some were too old, too out-of-shape, or simply unfit for service. In his novel, *The Private War of Jacket Coates,* the novelist Herbert Fairlie Wood invented a character who resembled some of the volunteers. "I have always been one to rally to king and country in an emergency," Coates says in the novel, "and in 1950 the emergency was that I was broke."

Fortunately, Canada had experienced leaders to instill discipline in the raw recruits. The brigade commander, John Rockingham, had served in the Second World War. He, in turn, appointed tough and experienced officers. One of them, Jacques Dextrase, said he didn't care if his men were "green as grass." He would train them to fight his way.

Canada's first brigade departed from Canada in November 1950 and January 1951. More contingents would follow.

KAPYONG

The first Canadian troops joined the line south of Seoul in February 1951. Their mettle soon was tested.

On April 22, Chinese troops broke through positions held by a South Korean division north of the Kapyong Valley. An Australian battalion on one side of the Kapyong River, and a Canadian on the other, were ordered to close the gap. Each dug into a hill and watched as the Koreans fled south in the valley between them.

The Australians were attacked at 10 p.m. on the night of April 23. Wave after wave of Chinese infantry piled onto their defences. They were fighting at close quarters in utter darkness. Only the light of overhead flares and flashes from enemy guns showed them where to shoot. The Chinese gave them no chance to bring artillery to bear: they were at the Australians' throats from the outset. No sooner was one wave repulsed than the next one rolled in. They fought all night and into the next day. Finally, as evening fell on April 24, the Australians pulled back. It was Canada's turn.

The battle to hold Hill 677 followed the same pattern. The Chinese came in waves. They seemed not to care about their own losses. They were determined to overwhelm the Canadian defenders by sheer weight of numbers, as they had overwhelmed the Koreans and Australians before them. If Hill 677 fell, the line would collapse: everything depended on the Canadians.

A platoon on the western side of the hill held its position. The Chinese swarmed up the northern slope and destroyed a second platoon. The first platoon was cut off and the battalion's headquarters was threatened. Just before dawn on April 25, the company commander made a difficult decision. He ordered his men to hunker down in their foxholes and called for an artillery bombardment on his own position. The barrage cut through the attackers. The hill was still surrounded, however, and the Canadians were running out of supplies. A perfect air drop in the morning kept the Canadians going and the line held.

The United States awarded the Princess Patricias a unit citation for the action at Kapyong. No other Canadian unit has been so honoured.

Soldiers from the Princess Pats cross a bridge, February 1951.
After the first year, Korea became a war of constant patrols.

THE HILLS

In its first year, the Korean War was a war of rapid movement. In its second year, it stood still. The Canadians, now part of the Commonwealth Division, engaged in regular patrols, fought off occasional Chinese attacks, and endured more or less regular artillery and mortar fire. By autumn 1951, the UN's defensive position had acquired a name: the Jamestown Line.

In November, the Chinese launched an offensive and Canadians fought in a number of significant engagements. On November 2, two companies of the RCR came under attack at Hill 187. Unlike earlier attacks, which had depended upon wave after wave of infantry, the Chinese now employed artillery. The barrage that came before the infantry assault was as heavy as some in the Second World War. The RCRs held their position. Later in the month, the Van Doos, under the command of Lieutenant-Colonel Jacques Dextrase, repelled a series of determined assaults by Chinese forces when the Americans withdrew from Hill 355, leaving the Canadian flank exposed. The Americans regrouped and returned the next morning.

THE LAST BATTLE

The war had reached a stalemate along Korea's 38th parallel. Negotiations meant to lead to a ceasefire began in the summer of 1951. These negotiations dragged on for years.

Serious skirmishes flared up periodically. In May 1953, all three Canadian battalions, under the command of Brigadier Jean-Victor Allard, successfully resisted another major Chinese assault on Hill 187. Terry Meagher, who witnessed the initial Chinese attack, described the scene vividly: "The place lit up; it was brighter than day. Grassfires broke out all over the valley and all over the hills; the minefield, wire, and trenches were destroyed. The bunkers caved in because the bombardment was so heavy. And the Chinese came in under the artillery barrage."

Two Canadian platoons were overrun. As in the earlier defence of Kapyong, a Canadian officer called in artillery fire on his own position. Some 4,000 shells rained down on the exposed attackers and the dug-in defenders. A combined force of RCR and Van Doos counterattacked, and the Chinese were chased back to their original position.

The Korean War is often referred to as a "police action" because it was fought officially with UN approval and the UN could not declare war. It was undoubtedly a war, however: both sides fought hard and both sides (and the civilian population) suffered.

Negotiations concluded finally in July 1953. Almost 27,000 Canadians had served in the conflict. More than 1,000 were wounded and 512 died.

FRONT LINE HOSPITAL

For every 1,000 Canadians who were wounded in the First World War, 114 died. The medical services provided to troops in the Second World War were more effective: for every 1,000 wounded, 66 died. In Korea, the figure was halved again: just 34 of every 1,000 perished because of their wounds.

The improvement had to do partly with the invention of antibiotic drugs. Penicillin, which first became widely available in the Second World War, saved many wounded men. The speed with which casualties were treated also improved their chances. Before the end of the Korean War, the Canadian Field Surgical Team was equipped to set up hospital facilities within helicopter range of the front lines—an enormous advance over anything that had been possible before.

Opposite page: Canadian artillery in action against the Chinese.

First UN peacekeepers to Middle East
May 1948

Lester Pearson awarded Nobel Peace Prize
December 1957

UN sends mission to Congo
July 1960

PEACEKEEPING

COLONIAL INHERITANCE

Before the Second World War, a number of European countries still occupied colonies in Africa, Asia, and the Middle East. In the years after the war, Britain got out of Palestine, India, and southern Africa; France got out of Indochina and Algeria; and Belgium got out of Rwanda and the Congo. Trouble often followed their withdrawal as different factions within the former colonies fought for control. Civil wars, insurrections, and wars of national liberation were among the legacies of European imperialism.

UNTSO AND THE BIRTH OF ISRAEL

In 1947, the United Nations passed a resolution calling for the creation of Israel. British forces, which had governed Palestine in the past, pulled out. The Arab countries in the region, whose leaders believed Palestine was theirs, attacked the new state of Israel. Gradually, however, the Israeli armed forces gained the upper hand. In 1949, the different countries signed an armistice and fighting ceased. The United Nations set up its first peacekeeping organization, the United Nations Truce Supervision Organization (UNTSO), to make sure the armistice was honoured by all sides.

Canadian soldiers patrol the line between Egypt and Israel in 1962.

AN IMPERIALIST PLOT

The UN observers in the middle east—who included Canadians—had a tough job. They occupied observation posts along the line that separated the opposing forces. When a skirmish occurred, the observers investigated and sent reports to the UN. Both sides often accused the observers of favouring their enemies.

A crisis occurred eight years after the creation of UNTSO. The strategically important Suez Canal, which was owned by a joint British and French company, linked the Mediterranean and the Red Sea. In July 1956, President Gamal Abdal Nasser directed Egyptian forces to take control of the canal. This outraged the British and French. The two countries conspired with Israel to bring about Nasser's downfall and reopen the canal. On October 29, Israel invaded Egypt's Sinai Desert on the eastern side of the canal. Egyptian forces fought back. A day later, Britain and France called on both sides to stop fighting and pull back their forces. Israel agreed, as planned. Egypt, which was being asked to pull its troops from the Suez Canal, refused, as expected. On October 31, the British and French joined in the attack against Egypt.

The two European countries thought the rest of the world would go along with their scheme. They were wrong. The Soviet Union, which had ties with Egypt, warned that their actions could lead to a wider war. The United States also opposed them. Even Canada was shocked. Lester "Mike" Pearson, Canada's minister of external affairs, made a speech at the UN intended to settle the crisis. He called on member countries to send a force "large enough to keep these borders at peace" until a political settlement was agreed on. The UN passed a resolution supporting Pearson's proposal on November 4, 1956.

THE RETURN OF SMILIN' SUNRAY

Canadian General E.L.M. Burns commanded UNTSO and its peacekeeping operation. The Canadian government offered to send the 1st Battalion of the Queen's Own Rifles. This was a mistake: the Egyptians had been on the point of going to war with the British. They were not prepared to tolerate troops named the "Queen's Own" on their territory, even if they were Canadian. Burns quietly recommended sending a mixed force of reconnaissance, signals, and administrative troops instead. In January 1957, the RCN aircraft carrier *Magnificent* set sail for the Middle East. On board were more than 1,000 officers and men, and equipment of the Royal Canadian Dragoons and Lord Strathcona's Horse. Lester Pearson was given the Nobel Peace Prize for his intervention at the UN and Canada's peacekeeping tradition was launched.

Lester B. Pearson

INCIDENT AT KISANDJI

The Canadians frequently found themselves in volatile situations. Early in 1964, Lieutenant-Colonel Paul Mayer and Sergeant J.A. Lessard of the Van Doos helped to rescue one hundred missionaries who were in danger of being murdered at Kisandji, Congo. Mayer negotiated with the chief of a group of armed rebels. The negotiations quickly took a crazy turn. One of the rebels threatened to chop off Mayer's finger unless he gave the rebel his wedding ring. Another rebel struck him on the back with the flat of his machete. Soon, the rabble was arguing over who would get to kill him. Mayer kept his cool and the missionaries (and Mayer) eventually were released. Both Mayer and Lessard were given the George Medal for bravery.

Right: Patrice Lumumba, leader of rebel forces in the Congo, is held by government soldiers in December 1960.
Inset above: Dag Hammarskjold covers his face with his hand during a debate in the Security Council in February 1961.

CONGO

Belgium had occupied the Congo in central Africa since the 1880s. When Belgium gave the Congo its independence in June 1960, the country erupted in violence.

The Congolese army mutinied against its mainly white officers. Some Belgian civilians were murdered and many others fled. The Congolese government asked for assistance first from the United Nations and then from the Soviet Union. The Belgian government sent in mercenaries. To make the situation even messier, the province of Katanga declared independence from the rest of the country.

In August 1960, the United Nations organized a peacekeeping force consisting mainly of African nations but also including Swedish, Irish, and Canadian troops. Their tasks were to make sure Belgian forces and mercenaries left the country; to assist the government in maintaining order; to end the civil war; and to preserve the Congo as a united country. ONUC (Organisation des Nations Unies au Congo) employed some 20,000 troops from more than 30 countries. They remained in the Congo for four years. UN Secretary-General Dag Hammarskjold and a popular Congolese leader, Patrice Lumumba, both died in the conflict. Hammarskjold was killed in an airplane crash; Lumumba disappeared after he was taken prisoner by Congolese troops. The way they died shows how difficult the conflict was. More than 200 UN troops also lost their lives.

THE CANADIAN CONTRIBUTION

Canada sent RCAF North Star aircraft to help deliver food to the Congo in July 1960. In September, 70 air force officers and support personnel assisted in operations against the Katangan rebels. French was the common language of Congo (another legacy of Belgian rule), but few of the nations serving with ONUC were bilingual. As a result, Canadians performed an essential role: by 1962, 16 bilingual Canadians occupied key positions on the ONUC staff. The chief Canadian contributions, however, were the signals units that provided vital radio communications across the Congo for the duration of the UN mission.

UNEASY PEACE IN CYPRUS

The beautiful Mediterranean island of Cyprus was given its independence by Britain in 1959. For a few years, the Greek majority and Turkish minority got along. Then, in 1963, the Greek leader, Archbishop Makarios, proposed changes to the island's constitution. The Turks objected to the changes. Some 500 people were killed in the riots and violence that followed. The Turkish government prepared to send troops to save its countrymen. The UN intervened.

The secretary general of the UN asked a number of countries to take part in the peacekeeping operation. In March and April 1964, Canada sent more than 1,000 troops to join the UN Force in Cyprus (UNFICYP). This was the first occasion on which a large Canadian infantry unit was placed between warring parties.

A battalion of Van Doos was among the first UN contingents on the island. Their reward for being first was the most dangerous assignment: they patrolled the Green Line that separated Greeks and Turks in the capital city, Nicosia, where enemies were a grenade's throw away from each other. When the Canadians were shot at, Makarios agreed that the buildings on either side of the Green Line should be cleared.

The Cyprus mission was peace*keeping* without peace*making:* the two sides remained opposed to each other for years. UNFICYP became an apparently endless operation. Canadian troops rotated through the island on a six-month cycle. Many Canadians served a number of tours of duty in Cyprus. They enjoyed the secluded beaches and seaside villages—when the two sides weren't shooting at each other.

INVASION!

In July 1974, Archbishop Makarios was overthrown. His place was taken by a Greek nationalist who was more virulently opposed to the Turks than his predecessor had been. Turkey responded by landing 40,000 troops on the island. They seized Nicosia and pushed some 200,000 Greek Cypriots out of their homes.

British and Canadian peacekeepers dug in around the airport to keep the Turkish forces from taking it over. Canadians also held the hotel in Nicosia that served as the Canadian headquarters. For a time, the situation was very tense. The British prime minister said later that Britain came "within an hour" of going to war with Turkey.

After the invasion, Canada increased its military commitment to UNFICYP. It helped to create a buffer zone across the entire island. Almost 20 years later, the two sides had not resolved their differences. Canada, fearing they never would, pulled out of UNFICYP in 1992.

RECCE PLATOON

Lewis MacKenzie, who later commanded Canadian troops in Yugoslavia, did a couple of tours in Cyprus. He remembered that the Turkish soldiers sometimes let their guard down, especially in the evenings, when they were apt to relax. MacKenzie, in charge of a reconnaissance ("recce") platoon, sometimes took advantage of their neglect. On one occasion, his platoon crept past a Turkish outpost in the middle of the night to establish an observation post (OP) on higher ground behind them. The assignment was not strictly necessary. It also was not without danger: the Turks might have shot them. But to MacKenzie and the Canadians the exercise served a number of purposes. It was obviously a good idea to have an OP in the best possible location. It sharpened the Canadians' skills. And it made the Turkish soldiers take them seriously.

Left: Turkish soldiers on patrol in Cyprus in 1964.
Inset above: A Canadian soldier raises the UN flag in Nicosia, Cyprus, March 1964.

VIETNAM

Vietnam had been a French colony. France pulled out when it was defeated by communist forces in 1954. Vietnam was cut in half after the conflict. The communists ruled North Vietnam. A republican government, supported by the United States, ruled the South. Communist guerrillas gradually stepped up their attacks on the republican government. By 1964, Americans were fighting alongside South Vietnamese troops to prevent a communist takeover. By 1968, there were half a million American soldiers in Vietnam. The war was the longest war fought by the United States. It was also their most crushing defeat.

Canada stayed out of the Vietnam War. However, many Canadians—perhaps as many as 20,000—fought as individuals in the United States armed forces. Canada also served on the International Control Commission (ICC) together with Poland and India. The job of the ICC was to monitor the peace agreement that had been signed in 1954. The task became meaningless as guerrilla attacks developed into a full-scale war.

When American troops withdrew from Vietnam in 1973, Canada was invited to join another mission to supervise the peace. The other members were Hungary and Poland (both communist) and Indonesia (which was neutral). In every incident they investigated, the communist members blamed South Vietnam, no matter what had really happened. Canada withdrew from the mission within a few months. The war ended with a communist victory in 1975.

American soldiers board a Chinook helicopter after an operation in the Shau Valley, Vietnam, in 1968. Thousands of Canadians served with American troops in Vietnam.

WHAT IT ALL MEANS

Les D. Brown was an 18-year-old Canadian living in California when he was conscripted into the United States Army. He learned what it was like to be a "grunt" (slang for infantry soldier) with the 1st Infantry Division in Vietnam in 1969. He also picked up the language of soldiers, the words and phrases they used to deal with their pain, disorientation, and fear. Two phrases he heard often were "It don't mean nothin'" and "There it is." The first phase could be applied to any situation, he wrote, "since nothin' meant nothin'. If a grunt found out he had to walk point that day, he could say, 'It don't mean nothin'.' The same phrase could be used if a grunt received no mail when others did. Any time a grunt complained or made a comment to another grunt, the second grunt could answer with 'There it is.' 'There it is' could mean 'Thanks for stating the obvious,' or 'I understand you, my brother, and feel what you feel.'"

A BRIDGE TOO FAR

Lewis MacKenzie, then a major with Canadian forces, served with the supervisory commission in Vietnam in 1973. On one occasion, he investigated the still-burning remains of a bridge, along with his Indonesian, Polish, and Hungarian colleagues. To MacKenzie and the Indonesian, it was obvious that the bridge had been destroyed by artillery fire. They could see shell holes in the ground. They also could calculate where the shells had come from: a North Vietnamese position about ten kilometres away. When they shared their findings with the Polish and Hungarian representatives, however, the communists disagreed. Absurdly, they insisted that the bridge had been blown down by the wind.

KUWAIT

On August 2, 1990, Iraq invaded its small, oil-rich neighbour, Kuwait. The United Nations condemned the aggression. The United States organized 35 countries in a coalition against Iraq. By late December 1990, the coalition had moved substantial forces into the region. After Iraq's leader, Saddam Hussein, ignored a final warning to withdraw from Kuwait, the coalition launched its attack.

Coalition planes flew devastating bombing missions against Iraqi targets beginning in January 1991. Then, on February 24, ground forces raced across the desert. They met only token resistance. Within three days, they had liberated Kuwait and seized Baghdad, the Iraqi capital. Saddam Hussein's government conceded defeat on March 3.

The coalition had agreed only to drive Iraq out of Kuwait. They had not signed on to topple the Iraqi leader. Saddam Hussein remained in power until the Second Gulf War, more than 12 years later.

ON PATROL AT SEA

The Canadian government was quick to join the American-led coalition. Two destroyers and the supply ship *Protecteur* were dispatched to the Gulf region in August 1990. Canadian forces, particularly the navy, had suffered in the preceding years from budget cuts. Programs to replace old equipment had been hung up by lack of money. Things were so bad that a gun supposedly was removed from a museum and fitted onto one of the ships before its departure. Still, the three vessels performed useful work in the Persian Gulf. They stopped and searched freighters suspected of carrying military supplies to Iraq. Encounters with smugglers were always tense and the operations had to be carried out aggressively and efficiently. By December, the Canadians had conducted roughly one-quarter of the inspections undertaken by the coalition fleet.

THE DESERT CATS

In October 1990, the Canadian government committed a squadron of CF-18 Hornet fighters based in Germany to the Persian Gulf. The planes, armed with guns and missiles, were capable of flying at 2,000 kilometres per hour. Two airfields, called Canada Dry One and Canada Dry Two, were constructed in Qatar. The pilots called themselves the "Desert Cats." Troops from the Royal Canadian Regiment defended their perimeters.

The Desert Cats patrolled the Gulf, where they strafed an Iraqi gunboat or two. When the coalition launched its attack, they bombed tanks, gun emplacements, and truck convoys. Often, the weather was so bad they saw nothing of their targets: computers guided their bombs to the ground. Altogether, more than 4,500 Canadians played a role in the Gulf War. It was Canada's first war since Korea and the first war in which women took part in combat.

Above: A Canadian CF-18 Hornet fighter in flight.
Left: Iraqi forces fleeing Kuwait were bombed relentlessly by coalition planes. The route to Iraq became known as the "Highway of Death."

Croatia, Slovenia
declare independence
June 25, 1991

Canadians sent to
former Yugoslavia
February 1992

Canadian Airborne Regiment
in Somalia
December 15, 1992

Rwandan genocide begins
April 6, 1994

NATO planes attack
Serb forces in Kosovo
March 24, 1999

Kosovo fighting ends
June 20, 1999

PEACE ENFORCEMENT

THE BREAKUP OF YUGOSLAVIA

After the Second World War, Josip Tito, a Croatian communist who had led a guerrilla campaign against the Germans, welded together seven republics (Serbia, Croatia, Bosnia-Herzegovina, Slovenia, Macedonia, and Montenegro) into a single communist state—Yugoslavia. Tito died in 1980. Less than a decade later, in 1989, the Soviet-led communist bloc of countries fell apart. Beginning in March 1991, the different republics of Yugoslavia came unstuck as well.

Some of the leaders who set out to make their states independent were driven by racial and religious hatred. They set loose private armies, some led by criminals, that quickly turned a civil war into a humanitarian catastrophe. The world learned the term "ethnic cleansing" in August 1991, when the village of Kijevo in Croatia was burned down by Serbian attackers. Its population was either murdered or forced to flee.

The UN negotiated the first of many ceasefire agreements in November. All were broken. Elements of the UN Protection Force (UNPROFOR) began to arrive in Bosnia and Croatia in January and February 1992. Canada sent more than 1,000 soldiers, police, and military personnel to the first contingent. Over the following three years, they did their best to deter the violence, protect civilians, and fight off attacks by private armies. This was never a true peacekeeping mission. The combatants did not want peace. UN forces were often ignored. Sometimes they were taken as hostages or used as a shield.

Canadian soldiers check out a car in Kosovo in July 1999.

THE INCIDENT AT MEDAK POCKET

In July 1993, Canadians led by Lieutenant-Colonel James Calvin were monitoring contested territory near the village of Medak. Serb and Croat forces were shooting at each other regularly. Sometimes, they used the Canadians as cover and the Canadians became targets. On September 9, the Croats mounted an all-out attack on the village. They used tanks, artillery, rocket-propelled grenades—everything they had. There were fires and explosions all around. Four Canadian soldiers were wounded by shrapnel while they attempted to do their job, which was to observe and report what was happening. The UN negotiated a cease-fire two days later. According to the agreement, the Croats would withdraw and the Canadians would occupy a buffer zone between the belligerents. The Canadians started moving in at the agreed time—but the Croats kept on shooting and the Canadians were forced to shoot back. Finally, the Croats did withdraw, but not until they had destroyed the village and killed many of its inhabitants.

TEENAGE HOODLUMS

"Let's say you took the City of Toronto, took away all the police, then gave every 16-year-old an AK-47 and an unlimited supply of ammunition and turned him loose. That's what you've got in Sarajevo. . . . In Sarajevo we were shot at every single day."

—Sergeant Jim Davis

A Canadian observer on a Bison armoured vehicle watches as Serb tanks drive by.

THE ROAD TO SARAJEVO

The city of Sarajevo was the site of the Winter Olympic Games in 1984. Less than a decade later, it was under siege by Bosnian Serbs. In June 1992, Canadian forces set out to secure the airport so that planes could land with supplies for the city's residents. Brigadier-General Lewis MacKenzie expected

trouble and equipped the Canadian contingent for combat, with mortars and anti-tank missiles. The operation was tense, as he had anticipated: three Canadian soldiers were wounded by snipers. The airport was secured, however, and four planes landed on June 30. The separate states of what once had been Yugoslavia continued to fight one another for years. The situation worsened in 1998 when Serbian forces invaded Kosovo. A peace agreement brought an end to the war in 1999. Canadian soldiers were still serving as peacekeepers in Kosovo a decade later.

THE SOMALIA AFFAIR

In the early 1990s, drought, famine, and conflict among different clans led to a breakdown of law and order in Somalia. Hundreds of thousands of people were in danger of dying of starvation or violence. In late 1992, the United Nations decided to send a substantial armed contingent to make the country safe, so that relief agencies could get food and other aid to the population. Canada's main contribution was to send the Canadian Airborne Regiment. It landed in Somalia in December.

Conditions were difficult. The dust and heat were often unbearable. Armed thugs in "technicals" (pickup trucks fitted with machine guns) roamed through the cities and towns. The Canadians built bridges, removed landmines, and escorted relief convoys. They reached out to the civilian population by building schools and offering medical services. Sadly, the Canadian effort was damaged when Canadian soldiers murdered a Somali youth. The Canadian government responded with drastic action, by disbanding the regiment. The UN mission to Somalia was shut down in 1995.

Years later, Somalia was still a country without an effective government. Starvation and strife continued to plague the population. The problems were too difficult to be solved by soldiers from other nations, however well-intentioned. The world was discovering that peacekeepers could only do so much.

A child, weakened by hunger, lies on the pavement in Mogadishu, capital of Somalia, in 1992.

THE RWANDAN GENOCIDE

Rwanda had been a Belgian colony. It became a republic in 1961. Its population was made up largely of two peoples, Hutu and Tutsi. Although they had lived together for many years, there was tension between them. Sometimes the tension became violence. Hutus dominated the government. They used their positions to harass the Tutsi minority. Some formed an extremist organization, the Hutu Power Movement, which called for all Tutsis to be killed. Meanwhile, hundreds of thousands of Tutsis crossed the border to Uganda. Some of these exiles formed a rebel army, the Rwandan Patriotic Front (RPF). In October 1990, the RPF invaded Rwanda, where they began a long struggle with the Rwandan military.

In August 1993, Rwanda and the RPF signed a peace agreement, the Arusha Accords. According to the agreement, Tutsi refugees would be allowed to return to Rwanda. The United Nations Assistance Mission in Rwanda (UNAMIR) was set up to make sure that the Accords were honoured. A Canadian officer, Brigadier-General Roméo Dallaire, took command of the UN contingent. Just 2,500 UN soldiers, mainly from Belgium and Bangladesh (not Canada), arrived in Rwanda in October.

On April 6, 1994, the Rwandan president was murdered. The government was taken over by extremist supporters of the Hutu Power Movement and the killings began. In the one hundred days that followed, 800,000 Tutsis were tortured and killed. Many were hacked to death by neighbours using machetes. Villagers were locked inside churches that were burned to the ground. Officials at the United Nations headquarters in New York were reluctant to believe the situation was as bad as Dallaire said and did not take the messages he sent to them seriously. They ordered him to co-operate with the government that was organizing the massacres. In the chaos and confusion, ten Belgian peacekeepers were killed.

The Rwandan genocide ended in July 1994 when the RPF took over the government. Three hundred and fifty Canadian troops arrived as part of the new UN force, UNAMIR II, that was set up after the catastrophe. By then, of course, the appalling damage had been done.

SHAKING HANDS WITH THE DEVIL

Roméo Dallaire reported later that he was in the presence of evil when he negotiated with the murderers. "They were devils," he told the Canadian Broadcasting Corporation. "And I couldn't see them as human. . . . They had erased themselves." He blamed himself for his own and the UN's failure to prevent the killings. He retired from the military and now works as a scholar focused on conflict resolution.

Above: General Roméo Dallaire.
Left: Thousands of Tutsis took shelter in the refugee camp in Goma, Zaire, across the border from Rwanda.

THE END OF PEACEKEEPING?

Canadian forces have served in peacekeeping operations in nearly 40 countries around the world. More than 120 have lost their lives in these overseas missions. Everywhere they go, they act with toughness towards belligerents and compassion towards civilians. An American general once told Lewis MacKenzie how much he appreciated the Canadian troops. They don't just go back to camp at the end of the day, he told MacKenzie. Instead, they go out and build a school, fix up an orphanage, improve the water supply. They build a bridge. If the bridge is destroyed in the night, they go back and build it again. It's the extra time the Canadians put in that makes them special, he said. They show other nations how the job should be done.

In recent years, Canada has participated in fewer peacekeeping missions than before. Operations that have gone badly, like those in Somalia and Rwanda, have shown that peacekeeping works only when there is peace to keep. Canada still makes a substantial contribution. Canadian observers monitor elections and ceasefire agreements in faraway countries. Specially equipped teams go in to help when disasters strike. A Canadian military team was among the first to respond to the earthquake in Haiti in 2010. But in the first decade of the twenty-first century, major peacekeeping operations were given a relatively low priority. Canadians went back to war.

Canadian troops scramble down from a helicopter in eastern Afghanistan.

9/11 AND AFTER

On September 11, 2001, terrorists hijacked four commercial airliners in the United States. They flew two of them into the World Trade Center in New York City, the third into the Pentagon in Arlington, Virginia, and the fourth crashed in Pennsylvania. The terrorists were members of al Qaeda, a Muslim extremist organization led by Osama bin Laden. Bin Laden hid in Afghanistan where the Taliban government supported his extremist program. The United States responded to the attacks by invading Afghanistan and overthrowing the Taliban government.

The United States helped to establish a new government in Afghanistan. The Taliban, however, was not finished. Taliban insurgents conducted guerrilla operations throughout the country. They were especially effective in mountainous regions where they were difficult to dislodge. The United Nations supported the United States in forming a coalition of countries to carry on the war. The International Security Assistance Force (ISAF) involved more than 40,000 troops from 39 countries. Canada was among the first countries to join.

FIGHTING WITH INTELLIGENCE

The Canadians and Americans sometimes demonstrated a different style of fighting. The Canadians planned their attacks after gathering intelligence and reports from reconnaissance patrols. They liked to know, if possible, what they were getting into. The Americans in some cases preferred a "run-and-gun" approach. If they saw a chance to attack, they went for it. On at least one occasion during Operation Medusa, a Canadian major opposed the decision of an American colonel to drive into Taliban-held territory. "I wanted to send reconnaissance across the night before to check the bank at the other side," the major explained, "to make sure we could actually get the vehicles up and over, because what's the use in trying to do an assault river-crossing if you can't get a toehold on the other side of the river?" The Canadian won this argument. The incident showed, however, that even close allies sometimes disagree.

Above: Canadians leave Camp Julien after handing it over to Afghan troops in November 2005.
Left: Canadian troops with a suspected terrorist head to their helicopter in Kandahar province.

FROM KABUL TO KANDAHAR

The first contingent of Canadian troops landed in Afghanistan in February 2002. From 2003 to 2005, they provided security in the capital city of Kabul. The operation was focused on improving the lives of Afghan civilians. Canadian soldiers and police trained their Afghan counterparts to fight the war and keep the peace on their own.

Beginning in 2006, Canada took on a much more difficult and dangerous task. It assumed leadership of the Provincial Reconstruction Team (PRT) in the southern province of Kandahar. Taliban guerrillas controlled much of the province. The Canadians provided a battle group. With their allies, they had more armour (tanks and APCs) and firepower than the enemy, and they controlled the sky. The Taliban countered these advantages by perfecting improvised explosive devices (IEDs)—powerful bombs hidden by the side of the road—and by terrorizing the Afghan police and civilians in sudden hit-and-run assaults.

The Taliban sometimes fought pitched battles in the open as well. Soon after the Canadians moved into Kandahar, they saw that Taliban forces were massing in the Panjwaii district. It was as if they wanted to test the Canadians, to see how ready they were for a fight. The coalition, led by the Canadian contingent, launched Operation Medusa to push back at the Taliban forces. The

Canadians were mainly from the Royal Canadian Regiment, supported by companies from the Princess Patricias and some specialized American units. The fighting reached a peak of intensity in early September 2006. The Taliban lost approximately 200 fighters while the Canadians lost 19. The fact that 11 Canadians were killed by direct fire revealed the kind of war they were engaged in. Most Canadian losses, before Operation Medusa and later, were caused by IEDs and suicide attacks.

THE CANADIAN COMMITMENT

In mid-2010, there were more than 2,800 Canadian troops in Afghanistan. One hundred and fifty Canadian soldiers had been killed there. It was, for Canada, yet another war in a faraway country. It was a real war, in which Canadians were being killed and were killing other soldiers, for a cause they believed to be just. The Canadian military contribution to ISAF was scheduled to end in 2011.

CANADIANS ALL

The Canadians who have fought our wars belong to us. They are part of what makes us Canadian. John Gallishaw, the corporal from Newfoundland who was pinned down by enemy fire on the beach at Gallipoli, is one of us. So are Laura Gamble, the nurse from Toronto who tended wounded soldiers in France; and Henry Louis Norwest, the Métis marksman from Saskatchewan who shot more than a hundred enemy soldiers; and Lucien Dumais, the Québécois who worked behind enemy lines to rescue Allied pilots; and Tommy Prince, whose exploits with the Devil's Brigade became legendary; and Lieutenant-Colonel Paul Mayer whose cool behaviour in a tense situation saved the lives of a hundred missionaries in the Congo.

They are a few of the hundreds of thousands of Canadians who have fought in wars and kept the peace around the world for more than 140 years. They are out there still. And they make us proud.

Left: Canadian troops open fire against a terrorist stronghold in Kandahar.
Above: Canadians line a stretch of the 401 highway, known as the "Highway of Heroes," to watch a motorcade bringing home a soldier killed in Afghanistan.

INDEX

(A date in parentheses following a place name indicates a significant Canadian operation.)

PICTURE CREDITS

The publisher gratefully acknowledges D.J. Goodspeed's *The Armed Forces of Canada 1867-1967* as a scholarly source for the maps included in this title.

FURTHER READING

General histories that all readers will find useful include:
D.J. Goodspeed, *The Armed Forces of Canada 1867-1967* (Queen's Printer, 1967); Desmond Morton, *A Military History of Canada*, Fourth Edition (McClelland & Stewart, 1999); David Bercuson, *The Fighting Canadians* (HarperCollins, 2008); J.L. Granatstein and Norman Hillmer, *Battle Lines: Eyewitness Accounts from Canada's Military History* (Thomas Allen, 2004); and Gwynne Dyer and Tina Viljoen, *The Defence of Canada: In the Arms of the Empire 1760-1939* (McClelland & Stewart, 1990). For background information, I drew on C.P. Stacey, *Canada in the Age of Conflict, Vol. 1* (Macmillan, 1977). David Bercuson, *Significant Incident* (McClelland & Stewart, 1996), although chiefly devoted to Canada's mission to Somalia, offers valuable insight into all things military.

The experience of Canadians in the First World War is well told in J.L. Granatstein, *Hell's Corner: An Illustrated History of Canada's Great War, 1914-1918* (Douglas & McIntyre, 2004) and Desmond Morton, *When Your Number's Up: The Canadian Soldier in the First World War* (Random House, 1993).

David Bercuson, *Maple Leaf Against the Axis: Canada's Second World War* (Stoddart, 1995) is a reliable overview. Marc Milner, *Canada's Navy: The First Century* (University of Toronto Press, 1999) is indispensable. Hal Lawrence, *A Bloody War: One Man's Memories of the Canadian Navy 1939-45*, if you can find it, is full of good stories. Everyone should read Farley Mowat's war books, including *The Regiment* (McClelland & Stewart, 1967), *And No Birds Sang* (McClelland & Stewart, 1979), and *My Father's Son* (Key Porter, 1992). For insight into the irreverence and independent spirit of the Canadian soldier (and for fun) try Earle Birney, *Turvey: A Military Picaresque*. Originally published by McClelland & Stewart in 1958, it is available in a New Canadian Library paperback edition.

Among other books consulted: J.L. Granatstein, *War and Peacekeeping: From the Boer War to the Gulf War, Canada's Limited Wars* (Key Porter, 1992); William Weintraub, *City Unique* (McClelland & Stewart, 1996) about Montreal in the war years; John Wood (ed.), *The Chance of War: Canadian Soldiers in the Balkans 1992-1995* (Dundurn, 2004); Lewis MacKenzie, *Peacekeeper: The Road to Sarajevo* (Douglas & McIntyre, 1993); and Les D. Brown, *There It Is* (McClelland & Stewart, 2000), a grim memoir by a Canadian in Vietnam.

There is, of course, a great deal of information on the internet. Among the most useful websites are those maintained by the Canadian War Museum, Canada's Department of Veterans Affairs, and *Legion* magazine.

ACKNOWLEDGEMENTS

Col. C.P. Stacey, who supervised my master's thesis at the University of Toronto long ago, was responsible, as much as anyone, for establishing a tradition of military-historical writing in Canada. His work, and that of the historians who have followed him, has been indispensable to me in researching this book.

The idea for *Canada's Wars* was Malcolm Lester's. Oliver Salzmann of Madison Press Books made it possible. I thank both of them for inviting me to be a part of it. Barbara Hehner, who was originally commissioned to write the text, generously shared her preliminary editorial work. Sharon Kish worked long, hard hours on the design and layout. To all at Madison and Scholastic who contributed their insight, skill, and time, my thanks.

My thanks, also, to Professor J.L. Granatstein, who reviewed the text and generously contributed the Foreword.

Text, design and compilation © 2010 the Madison Press Limited

Library and Archives Canada Cataloguing in Publication

Webb, Jonathan, 1950–
Canada's wars : an illustrated history / Jonathan Webb.

ISBN 978-0-545-98026-5

1. Canada—History, Military—Juvenile literature.
2. Canada—Armed Forces—History—Juvenile literature.
3. Canada—Armed Forces—Biography—Juvenile literature.
I. Title.

FC226.W43 2010   j355.00971   C2010-902613-6

Canada's Wars was produced by Madison Press Books
1000 Yonge Street, Suite 303
Toronto, Ontario, Canada
M4W 2K2

Design, layout and map illustration: Sharon Kish
Copy editor: Lesley Fraser
Index: Ruth Pincoe
Production manager: Brendan Davis
Publisher-at-large: Malcolm Lester
Publisher: Oliver Salzmann

OGP 10 9 8 7 6 5 4 3 2 1
Printed in China

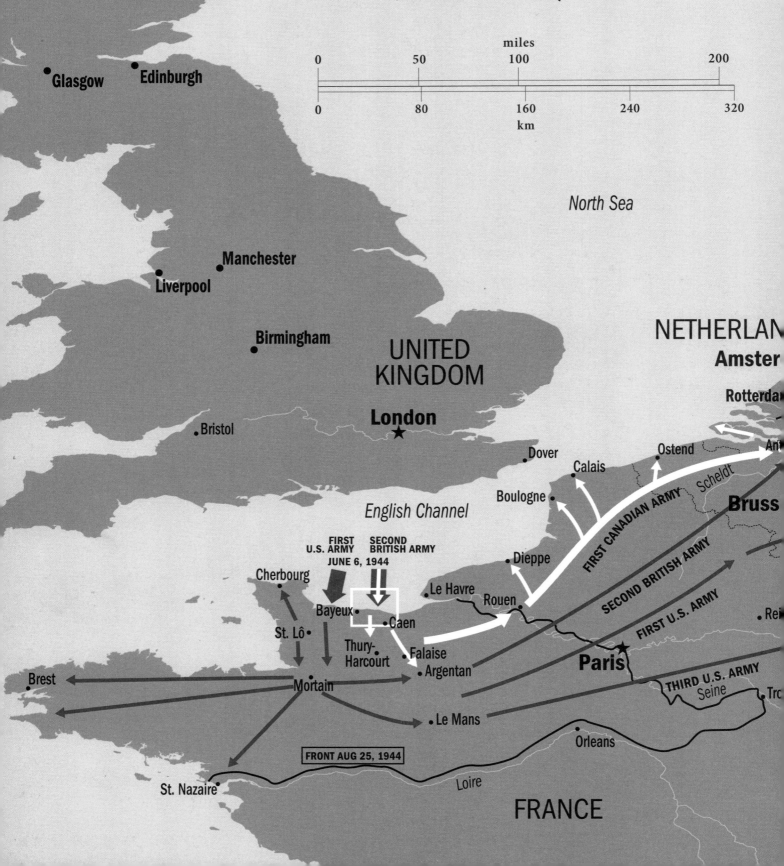

VICTORY IN EUROPE
June 6, 1944–May 8, 1945

miles
0   50   100   200

0   80   160   240   320
km

Glasgow   Edinburgh

North Sea

Manchester
Liverpool

Birmingham

NETHERLAN
Amster

Rotterda

UNITED
KINGDOM

London

Bristol

Dover

Calais
Boulogne

Ostend

An

FIRST CANADIAN ARMY

Scheldt

Bruss

English Channel

Dieppe

SECOND BRITISH ARMY

FIRST
U.S. ARMY
JUNE 6, 1944

SECOND
BRITISH ARMY

Le Havre

Rouen

FIRST U.S. ARMY

Cherbourg

Bayeux

Caen

Re

St. Lô

Thury-
Harcourt

Falaise

Argentan

Paris

Brest

Mortain

THIRD U.S. ARMY

Le Mans

Seine

Tro

Orleans

FRONT AUG 25, 1944

St. Nazaire

Loire

FRANCE